ARCHIPELAGO NEW YORK

ARCHIPELAGO NEW YORK

THOMAS HALACZINSKY

Schiffer Publishing Ltd®

4880 Lower Valley Road · Atglen, PA 19310

Other Schiffer Books on Related Subjects:

Lighthouses of New York, Rick Tuers, ISBN 978-0-7643-2692-9

Vista Manhattan: Views from New York City's Finest Residences, Mike Tauber, ISBN 978-0-7643-5148-8

New York Subway Graffiti, Tod Lange, ISBN 978-0-7643-3339-2

Designed by Brenda McCallum

Maps provided by NOAA Office of Coast Survey, nauticalcharts.noaa.gov. More information on how copyrights apply to government publications can be found at US Government Works.

Back cover: photo by Adam Nawrot

Type set in Avenir/Minion

ISBN: 978-0-7643-5507-3

Printed in China

Published by Schiffer Publishing, Ltd.
4880 Lower Valley Road | Atglen, PA 19310
Phone: (610) 593-1777; Fax: (610) 593-2002
E-mail: Info@schifferbooks.com | Web: www.schifferbooks.com

For our complete selection of fine books on this and related subjects, please visit our website at www.schifferbooks.com. You may also write for a free catalog.

Schiffer Publishing's titles are available at special discounts for bulk purchases for sales promotions or premiums. Special editions, including personalized covers, corporate imprints, and excerpts, can be created in large quantities for special needs. For more information, contact the publisher.

We are always looking for people to write books on new and related subjects. If you have an idea for a book, please contact us at proposals@schifferbooks.com.

CONTENTS

NEW HAVEN

NEW YORK

Bridgeport

Falkner I.

(use chart 12354)

S Norwalk

L O N G   I S L A N D

Stamford

NEW JERSEY

Hudson R.

New Rochelle

(use chart 12363)

Eatons Neck

Port Jefferson

R TRS
(WHRF)
1570 kHz ⊙

NEW YORK

Sands Pt.

Oyster Bay

R TRS
⊙ (WGSM)
740 kHz

Shin
B

L O N G   I S L A N D

AERO Rot W&G

R TR
(WALK)
1370 kHz

JERSEY
CITY

BROOKLYN

Jamaica Bay

AERO
Rot W&G

R TR
(WGBB)
1240 kHz

GREAT   SOUTH   BAY

PA

RW "M"
Mo (A)
WHIS 15

13

15   1

aten I

AERO R Bn 373 (⁻⁻⁻⁻)

LIGHTED TOWER

Obstn
Fish Haven
(auth min 8 fms)

S

11   14

13

18   18

Fire I Inlet

FIRE ISLAND
Fl 7.5s 167ft 24M

14   17

Jones Inlet

E Rockaway

Obstn PA
(6½ fms rep) 12

Y"W"
Fl Y 4s
Priv

15   19

Rockaway
Beach

12   13

19   20   21   2

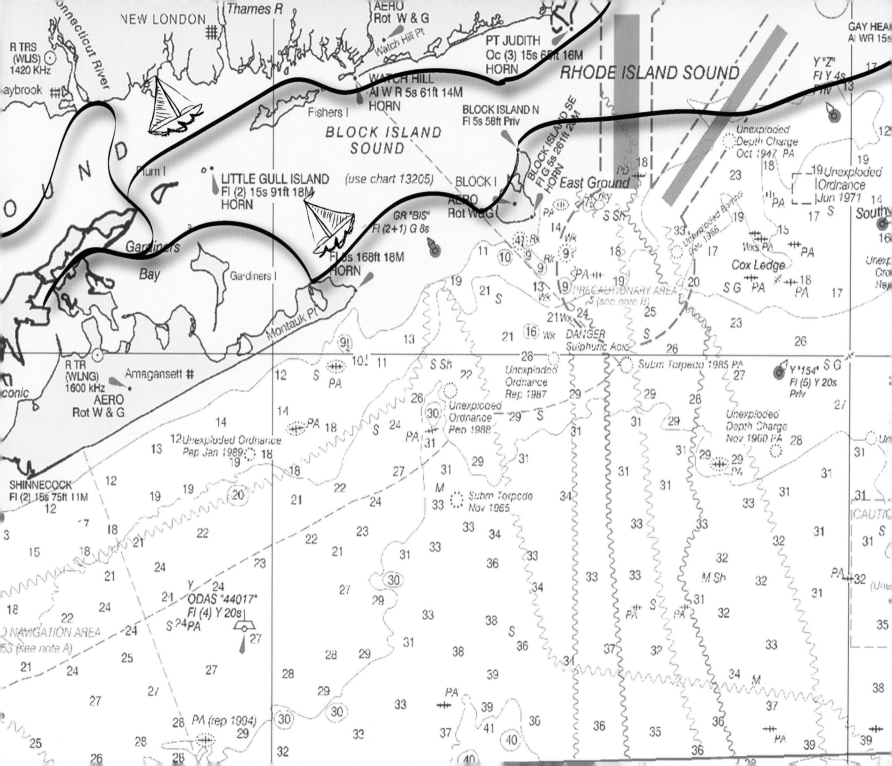

143

126

97
G S

89

-93

S St

34
22

erry
Pt   Orl

7   3

16
Shellfi
n t 7 PA
19   h
o   1(

19   1!
Shellfish rac
(auth min 10l
14 h
6"

15
ast Fl 4
PA

G   h
"3" 74
10
OLREGS D.
30.155e
4

12

13
2
1
ulture

6

B (rep.2003)
+5 (rep
1 7
4 6

P R E F A C E

When I first arrived in Manhattan from Europe in the early 1990s, I was surprised to find that most New Yorkers were either unaware they were living on an island, or didn't care. The city's waterfront was neglected, the old docks on the west side were dilapidated, and access to the water was cut off by major highways to the east and west.

For me as a newcomer, no place was too far off the beaten path to explore. Like the water gazers in Herman Melville's *Moby Dick*, standing at the Battery and looking out onto the Atlantic Ocean filled me with a sentiment that's hard to describe. It wasn't the longing for home or Heimweh — as it might be called in my native German—but much more the desire to connect with the place I had arrived at.

In 2012, I finally managed to get my own boat, an old thirty-foot sloop outfitted for single-handed sailing. Gliding for the very first time into the New York Harbor and passing the Statue of Liberty, I suddenly understood: nobody arrives on an island in the true sense of the word unless by boat.

Charting a route virtually identical to that of Adriaen Block, the Dutch Explorer who in 1614 first sailed up the East River into Long Island Sound and charted the territory, calling it an archipelago, I realized that I was doing more than discovering a territory. The farther out to sea I ventured, often alone, the more this modern-day exploration of New York's mysterious islands turned into an inner journey, a quest for identity and sense of place.

The way nature and the urban environment coexist in New York's archipelago inspired my photography. Images of the city glimmering like a Fata Morgana over the marsh in Jamaica Bay tell their own story. The sea is an empty canvas on which the reflection of the sky, the changing light, the mist, and fog paints its pictures. Time is reflected in each image of the space around me. Images and stories complement each other in this existential experience, and so the photographs in this book are not illustrative of the stories told, and the tales don't explain the depiction.

Arriving on the island of Manhattan not only changed my perspective of the city, but also my life, so naturally the story of approaching New York from the water had to be the last chapter of the book.

This journey would have not been possible without the help and support of many people who crossed my path, told me a story, or listened to my questions. My sincere gratitude to them all, including first and foremost Petrina Engelke, who started to sail with me and became my wife along the journey; this would not have been the book it is without her. Peter Hampel, who joined me on many legs of the voyage, taught me so much about sailing and became a most trusted companion; Jacques Menasche, my first editor who encouraged me and helped me to find a voice; Professor William Kornblum, who through his book, *At Sea in the City*, inspired me on this journey and helped me get the facts right. Lastly, I want to thank Cheryl Weber and my publisher, Schiffer Books, for believing in this project and bringing this book into the world.

ISLANDS ALL AROUND

My last night at home had been comfortable. The air conditioner had cooled the room to seventy-two degrees and kept the humid New York summer night outside. It was a different story on the boat. Despite the open hatches, the air was stagnant and, though the sun had long set, the heat lingered in every cranny. There was no one to talk to, and I was too excited to sleep. I was sailing to places I could easily reach by car in less than an hour, but it was an adventure and a challenge. Recently, not too far from here, the boat of two well-seasoned fishermen had capsized and they had drowned.

I had spent the whole day hauling food and supplies on board the *Sojourn*. Now it was all neatly stowed away. The batteries were charged and the water tank filled. I was ready for the trip I had been dreaming of since first arriving in the most famous city in the world.

Long ago I had fallen in love with the old nautical charts of this part of the Eastern Seaboard. They had revealed an archipelago that rivaled, in size and beauty, Venice, Istanbul, and Hong Kong. By "archipelago" I mean more than a geographical description of a group of islands. I mean it poetically. It's what the ancient Greek poet Homer had called the Aegean Sea—the aquatic stage of Odysseus' long journey home. That very same sea, now the drowning ground of thousands of refugees, turns through the Strait of Gibraltar and pours into the Atlantic Ocean where my little plastic boat is at this moment bobbing. The five oceans of the planet are all connected.

I rolled out the nautical chart where I plotted my journey. There were islands everywhere. Within a 140-nautical-mile radius I counted at least seventy, some large and inhabited, some abandoned and left to nature, and some too small to live on. A few were now connected to each other through landfill, like Long Island to Brooklyn's Barren Island. Tomorrow would be a long day. I rolled up the chart, switched off the light, and eventually fell asleep.

The screeching cry of a seagull woke me at dawn. When I stepped on deck, a hot cup of coffee in hand, there was already a commotion on the dock as a group of Chinese fishermen prepped their boat for the day. Most boat owners here at the Gateway Marina in Brooklyn are white middle-class men for whom fishing is a hobby. But in the last couple of years, a new group has become a regular fixture at the marina: those who developed fishing into a small side business to survive financially, and even some who, unable to afford New York's rising rents, had taken to living on their boats full-time.

I turned on the old marine diesel, untied my lines, and within minutes I was on my way. Getting out of the Gateway Marina, I carefully maneuvered around a sand bank and into deeper water where I could set the sail. I was in no rush. I ran the motor on a low speed and slowly made my way into Dead Horse Bay. There was a light southwest morning breeze and, three hours after low tide at the Battery, a good current to ride toward Breezy Point. This morning the bay seemed pleasant and, if you didn't know any better, placid. But while today it is part of the Gateway National Recreation Area, Dead Horse Bay was once the worst dumping ground in New York. For more than fifty years, between 1880 and 1930, more than two dozen factories hummed along, churning horse carcasses into soap, glue, and fertilizer. Whatever was left was dumped right into the water. Meanwhile, Barren Island, site of Floyd Bennett Field, New York's first airport, had been enlarged by more than 800 acres of landfill, mainly city garbage that even a century later continued to cough up bottles and other urban archeological artifacts onto Dead Horse Bay's deserted beaches.

At buoy 20, I turned the boat into the wind, arrested the wheel, and pulled up the main sail. No matter how many times I did it, shutting off the engine was always a magical moment. Suddenly, I heard nothing but the sound of the wind and the boat gently pushing through the water.

I was in no rush. I ran the motor on a low speed and
slowly made my way into Dead Horse Bay.

Looking out onto the open sea and the sandy beaches of Breezy Point on the port side, I saw no more traces of civilization; I had left the beach houses behind. It wouldn't have looked too different when Henry Hudson first set anchor here—September 6, 1609. That day, Robert Juet, Hudson's first mate, noted the shore party's report in his log book: "The land they told us was very pleasant with grass and flowers and goodly trees as ever they had seen and very sweet smells came from them." However, the first contact between Europeans and native New Yorkers was not as peaceful as described. On the very same day, the second mate of Hudson's ship *Half Moon*, an Englishman named John Colman, was trapped by a group of Algonquians and killed by an arrow shot into his throat.

Slowly approaching Breezy Point, the western most tip of the Rockaway peninsula, I passed a bell buoy whose random gong would guide me home should a sudden fog make any other orientation impossible. I had no need of the ringing at this particular moment, but it had a calming effect, part of a wider concert of sounds that encapsulated me on the boat. Sounds are an essential part of being on the water, and my ears are always attuned to the slightest variation in the tune. The pitch of the bow cutting through the water tells me how fast I am going, and I can gauge the wind from the sound of the airflow on the sail. The moaning of the standing rigging, the rattling of the halyards on the mast, and the sound of the lines stretching gives me an idea of the stress the boat is suffering under full sail. Right now, there was none; as I prepared to turn into the open ocean the wind hardly filled the sail. Looking southeast I saw the sea touch the sky on the horizon, the most beautiful nothingness one can imagine, only the glassy surface of the water blending seamlessly into the blue sky.

Looking out onto the open sea and the sandy beaches of Breezy Point on the port side,
I saw no more traces of civilization; I had left the beach houses behind.

IN THE JAW OF THE WHALE

A fresh southwest wind brought me back to the mouth of Dead Horse Bay earlier than expected, and with hours of sunlight left I decided to enter the marshland of Jamaica Bay, an estuary covering about 25,000 acres of wetland spanning the northwest shore of the Rockaway peninsula to Canarsie, Brooklyn.

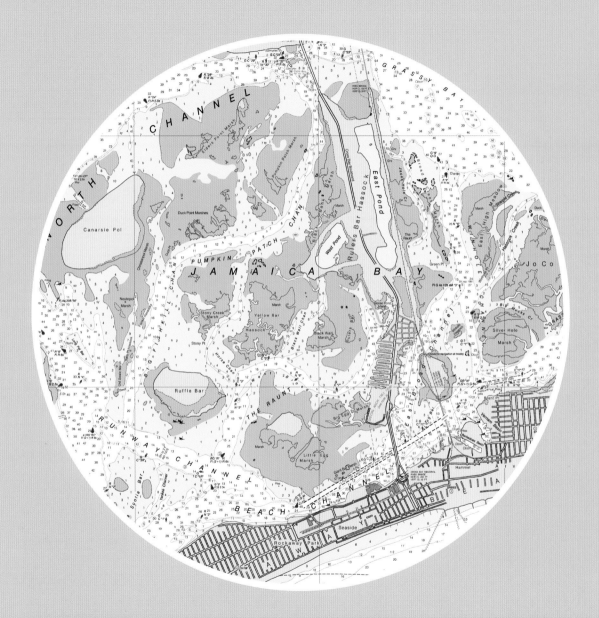

Propelled by the wind and a strong current, I was flying under the Marine Parkway-Gil Hodges Memorial Bridge at six knots. From above, the echo of car tires on the metal surface sounded like thousands of bees. Looking up, the tip of the mast seemed just about to scrape the underbelly of the bridge. I knew there was plenty of space, but I luffed to lean the boat even more. The intense humming, the blustery wind, and the boat cutting through the swell were a rush. Now, entering Jamaica Bay, I had to fall off. In a flash I let the main sheet out and slowed down to negotiate the shallower water of the bay.

Because my depth finder alarm had broken a long time ago, my eyes were glued to the digits jumping up and down on the gauge as I glided along Ruffles Bar and Little Egg Marsh under full sail. The navigational channels were sufficiently deep for a small craft like the *Sojourn*, but veering even slightly off track would pull me into troubled waters.

The waterway I was using is called Runway Channel. It cuts a straight line to New York's JFK landing strip at the far north end of the bay. When the airport was built in the 1940s, then called Idlewild, large areas of this inlet were dredged to make the bay navigable for the barges delivering building materials. Sediment from the estuary was then used to create land for the new aviation hub. It was an era when the legendary city planner Robert Moses was busy plastering the shorelines of New York and Brooklyn with concrete highways, and no one much cared about the effect on the marshland ecosystem.

I rolled in the genoa to slow the boat and hovered on the edge of the islands. Jamaica Bay's beaches gleamed golden in the afternoon sun, and the receding water of the low tide brought out the lush green of the marsh. Besides Ruffle Bar, there are a few more little islands with names like Goose Creek and Elders Point. Some of them disappear under water at high tide, and six hours later a totally different landscape surfaces. On the horizon I glimpsed the skyline of Manhattan with its new World Trade Center, visible on a clear day from thirty miles.

In a way, two worlds face each other at this place—the modern city skyline and an ancient Mannahatta that I could see, smell, and hear right in this bay between Brooklyn and Queens.

In a way, two worlds face each other at this place—the modern city skyline and an ancient Mannahatta that I could see, smell, and hear right in this bay between Brooklyn and Queens.

In the Lenape language the Rockaway Peninsula hugging the wetland was called *Reeckwackie*—which either translates as "the sandy land" or "the land of our people." "Jamaica" comes from *yameco*—land of the beaver. The Lenape were avid boaters, fishing and harvesting oysters and clams. They lived peacefully with the land and imagined Long Island as a big fish, a whale with its tail pointing east and its jaw at Rockaway Point.

It all changed when the Dutch and the British came in the 1600s. Even back then it was all about real estate. The colonists divided the island into parcels, and for the Natives the word mortgage became what it literally meant in its original French: a death pledge. The new European landowners claimed a tax from the Natives and in return promised to protect them from their enemies. When the Natives didn't want to pay, the director of the Dutch Colony, Willem Kieft, had his troops attack their villages, slaughtering men, women, and children. He blamed the Mohicans for the massacre, but the lie didn't stick; the tribes united and fought back, and 1643, became known as the Year of Blood.

It was right here, at the north shore of the Rockaway Peninsula, that sixteen chiefs of the Long Island tribes offered peace to the Dutch. "When you first arrived you were destitute for food; we gave you our beans, our corn, we fed you with oysters and fish and now for our recompense you murder our people," is how one chief addressed the Dutch. Even so, the Natives ultimately offered the invaders costly presents, brokering a short-lived peace agreement before the fighting resumed for another three years.

The navigational channels were sufficiently deep for a small craft like the Sojourn,
but veering even slightly off track would pull me into troubled waters.

The boat slowed dramatically. The wind had died and the sun began to set. The light pink sky intensified the green of the marsh. Fittingly, this area is also called the Irish Riviera. The name is often applied to Breezy Point and Rockaway Beach, but it is here, on the bay side toward Far Rockaway, that the Irish settled in the late 1800s, to found a vibrant fishing community. Hardworking, blue collar folks whose little frame houses in the marsh, built on stilts, are still here.

Today the little fishing boats all around me are captained by subway operators, mailmen, or plumbers who work on the million-dollar homes on Rockaway Beach during the day but then take refuge in New York's last marshland.

When it was almost time to take down the sail and motor back to my berth, my eye caught sight of the blue letters, *Jamaica Bay Guardian,* on an open white motorboat belonging to Don Riepe, one of the bay's unsung heroes.

During his twenty-five years as a manager of the National Park System, Don observed firsthand the disappearance of 1,600 acres of marshland. Realizing that this would eventually turn the bay into a stagnant, dead body of water, he became an environmental activist.

He tirelessly campaigned for saving the marshland, a natural habitat for hundreds of different bird species, until the Army Corps of Engineers finally agreed to restore the marsh to its pre-1970 state, using sediment from the deepening of New York Harbor. As the president of the Northeast Chapter of the American Littoral Society, Don continues to educate people about the importance of the marsh. He has inspired countless volunteers to help plant and maintain this precious nature sanctuary between Brooklyn and Queens.

I waved to Don, turned the boat, and started to sail back home.

OVERNIGHT IN LITTLE CUBA

Last night the weather changed suddenly, and I didn't return to safe harbor. Instead, I sailed under the Cross Bay Veterans Memorial Bridge and entered another world.

Dark clouds had turned the red sky into a steel-gray blanket, hanging heavy over the water. A rolling thunder, still far away, posed no immediate danger but promised a drenching before I could make it back to the marina. I decided to change course. A few hundred yards before the drawbridge ahead of me—built for the Long Island Railroad but now part of the New York City subway system—I turned to starboard and sailed into a narrow creek. Lined with stilt houses, Broad Channel Island, Jamaica Bay's only inhabited islet, has been known by many names at different times to the clam diggers and fishermen who lived here: Big Egg Marsh, Venice, or Little Cuba.

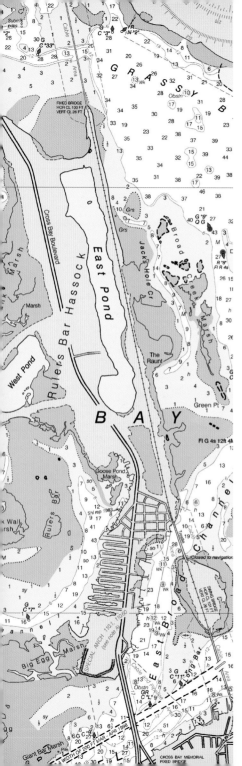

Time to get the motor started and the main sail down. I was heading to Iroquois Yacht Club at the waterway's narrow end, a magnificent name for what was just a small dock and boat shack. I'd spent a few weeks in a neighboring house the previous summer, and I knew some of the moorings were abandoned. I'd tie up there for the night. Hooking the boat to the floating white ball by myself was tricky. I made the approach carefully under motor and when I was so close to the mooring that I couldn't see it from the helm, I shifted into neutral, arrested the wheel, and let the boat float. I jumped quickly onto the foredeck, boat hook in hand, fished for the marker, caught it on the first try, and fastened the attached, wet bowline to the cleat.

I made it into the cabin just in time. As I pulled the hatch shut over my head, the wind blew harder and the thunder boomed louder and closer. The rain started to pound down like drumsticks on an empty barrel. Through the open window I saw the lightning dancing on the pitch-dark sky. A thunderstorm is always dangerous on the open water. I was happy to be safe, moored in a little bay next to one of my favorite islands in the archipelago. The wind gusts were pulling the boat hard, but the 300-pound base sitting in the muddy ground kept it fastened in place. Time for a glass of wine and getting cozy in the belly of the boat.

Half an hour later it was all over. A damp mist hung above the marsh, and the light of the setting sun brought the red back into the sky. I sat on the deck. If it wasn't for the muffled sound of the subway cars crossing the bridge less than a quarter of a mile away or the low-flying jumbo jets approaching JFK, I could have thought myself near a secluded island in a different era.

For many decades, the people who lived on this island respected the weather. Instead of trying to keep nature's force at bay, they built and lived in houses that could survive the rising water, and the soft marsh eventually absorbed the swells of the storm like a sponge. The fishermen's wisdom, gained through centuries of living with the water, inspired the award-winning architectural concepts developed in the aftermath of 2012's Hurricane Sandy to protect cities from rising sea levels and storm surges. Granted that Broad Channel has seen its share of devastation and been reshaped by its many storms, but the basic principles of protection remain successful: building structures are mainly made out of simple, readily available materials like wood from nearby trees. That way, a house washed into the sea can be replaced at a reasonable cost. After Hurricane Sandy, those islanders who failed to heed this wisdom faced financial ruin, victims of real estate prices disproportionate to construction value, and the reluctance of insurance companies to honor homeowners' policies.

It was a quiet evening and the water was as smooth as a mirror. Only the occasional airplane disturbed the tranquility, shooing away a plover or sandpiper. The Audubon Society has counted more than 300 different bird species, their nesting habitat long predating the arrival of the first white settlers. They first came to Little Marsh Egg after the Long Island Railroad had been built in the 1880s, to connect the island with Brooklyn and Queens. In time the area became known as the Venice of New York. The City Department of Docks and Ferries took control of the bay in 1904, and proposed to turn it into a commercial port—an act that sparked fierce opposition. The locals ultimately succeeded in forcing the city to withdraw the plan, but the island remained torn between work and play, fishermen versus vacationers from the city. Today, 2,000 people live on Broad Channel, a tightly knit community shaped by a long tradition of perseverance and reluctance to change.

During Prohibition in the 1920s, the island discovered a new identity as Little Cuba, a seaside resort without a police precinct, the perfect speakeasy getaway. Rum runners roamed between the islands and delivered the illicit drink to nearby hotels and resorts, and to dance halls and cabarets with entertainment by Jimmy Durante or Mae West, brimming with tourists and locals alike. Some of the houses on the water still have hatches in the floor, once used to secretly unload rum directly from the boats.

Today, 2,000 people live on Broad Channel, a tightly knit community shaped by a long tradition
of perseverance and reluctance to change.

Because Broad Channel Island was owned by the city of New York, for decades those living and working there couldn't own the plots their houses were built on. Instead, the land was leased to a tenant association, and when the contract expired in the 1940s, Robert Moses, park commissioner under Mayor Fiorello La Guardia, sought to demolish every standing structure on the island and turn the whole area into a wildlife preserve. Broad Channel Island, Moses argued, had become a slum. Fighting back, the islanders launched a well-orchestrated public relations campaign. They exposed the city's deceptions, including the use of images taken after a storm to show an island in decay. Moses, beaten, was forced to sell the land to the islanders, but it was a slow process and it wasn't until 1982, that Broad Channel Island residents were finally able to buy the parcels on which they had built their houses.

It was almost dark, and the scent of barbecue wafted over from the terrace of the Iroquois Yacht Club. Families that have lived here for generations were enjoying themselves after a long workday. But the peaceful atmosphere was deceptive; the island's days are numbered. Scientists are predicting that the New York sea level will rise by six feet over the next seventy-five years and that Broad Channel Island will slowly disappear.

I poured myself another glass of wine and watched the big red sun until its last rays sank into the water.

TO THE BEACH FOR A NICKEL'S FARE

I still hadn't seen a whale or dolphins. I was sailing north by northwest along Coney Island, where humpback whales are often found, and someone reported a dolphin sighting over the marine radio. I was on the lookout. Cruising at four to five knots, passing the random red or blue lobster trap buoy on the way, alone on board, there wasn't much to do. Even without the autopilot, the *Sojourn* was almost sailing herself, leaving me with nothing but the occasional course correction.

On the way to New York's lower bay into the Narrows, the tower of the parachute jump on the starboard side looked like a huge umbrella whose fabric had been ripped off in a hurricane. Originally an attraction at the 1930s World Fair in Flushing, Queens, the red structure, long in a state of disrepair, now stood with the Wonder Wheel and the Cyclone roller coaster, icons of the poor man's playground.

Still the closest escape from the city on a hot summer day for many New Yorkers, the beach was packed all the way from the amusement parks of Coney Island to Brighton Beach. I remembered how I felt watching the sailboats go by from there. It was the same beach where my dream to sail this coast was born.

On the water, propelled only by natural forces, I felt connected with all the sailors, seafarers, and explorers who had sailed these waters before. Heading toward the Verrazano-Narrows Bridge, I thought of its Italian namesake, Giovanni da Verrazzano, who sailed into the New York Bay on April 17, 1524, the first European ever to set foot on the island of Manhattan. Verrazzano, on a mission financed by France's King Francis, reported that he had christened the bay *Santa Margarita*, after the king's sister.

From the shore I could hear the faint music of the rides. Even with my eyes shut, I always knew when I was close to Coney. I heard the rattling of the old wooden roller coaster and the screaming passengers. I even thought I smelled hot dogs, cotton candy, and funnel cake, but maybe that was just my imagination.

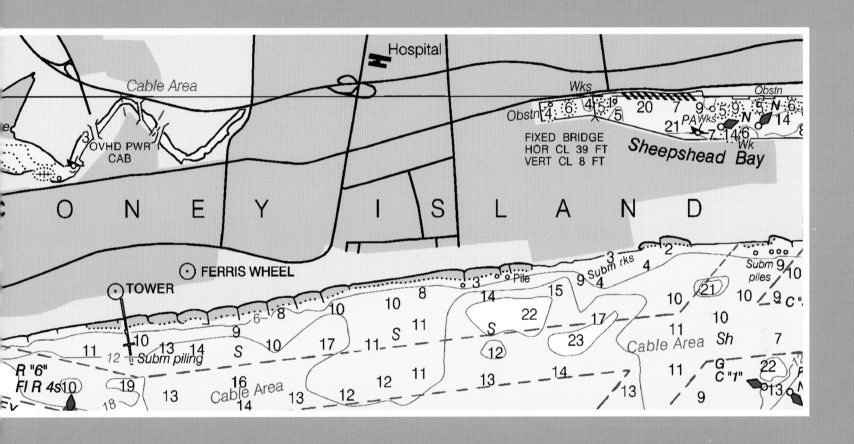

This island has been a place of fun and recreation from its early days. The Dutch, who used it as a favored hunting ground, like the British after them, called it *Konijn Hok,* rabbit's breeding place. When the Long Island Railroad was built in the late 1800s, workers filled the narrow stream that separated this place from Brooklyn, and the island turned into a peninsula. Reachable by land, it soon became a vacation and entertainment hot spot for New York's rich and famous. But in 1911, the Coney Island of the Gilded Age ended in a spectacular fire. Then, four years later, an extension of the New York subway started to bring thousands to the beach for a nickel's fare. The exclusive hotels where the Vanderbilts and Morgans used to vacation were replaced by roller coasters and shoot-the-chutes rides, The Tickler and Professor Wormwood's Monkey Theater, Steeplechase and Luna Park.

The wind, now blowing from the south, brought me quite close to the fishing pier that extends more than 1,000 feet into the sea. Fishing rods were hooked into the railing and loud music was playing from boom boxes. I had to luff to get farther away and pulled in the genoa sail a bit more. The boat leaned a little and elegantly passed the crowd. They waved and cheered me on.

In 1964, Donald Trump's father, Fred, built seven buildings with 3,800 rental and cooperative apartments. Convinced that the days of the amusement parks had come to an end, Trump famously organized a "funeral," inviting bystanders to demolish the stained windows of the remaining pavilions with stones handed out by girls in bikinis, before bulldozing them to the ground. But the amusement district survived and rose phoenix-like from the ashes. Rides and sideshow attractions continue to entertain a never-ending stream of New Yorkers, even today.

The boat leaned a little and elegantly passed the crowd. They waved and cheered me on.

TAKING A WALK ON THE PEOPLE'S BEACH

I could barely see the end of the dock. The fog was unusually dense for early October, and going out to sea without a radar on board, I would have to determine the proximity of other boats from their horns. This could get very confusing and eerie. I decided it would be better to stay in the harbor.

In spite of modern technology, seasoned skippers still stick to old rules that have regulated life on the water for millennia. Unlike most landlubbers, sailors don't rely solely on modern technology, particularly on a sailboat. The idea is to be self-sufficient, and dependence on batteries or a motor isn't smart. Although most modern boats are equipped with a GPS and computers, most skippers have paper charts, a parallel ruler, and a fixed-point divider on board. Experience, knowledge, and seamanship are what counts.

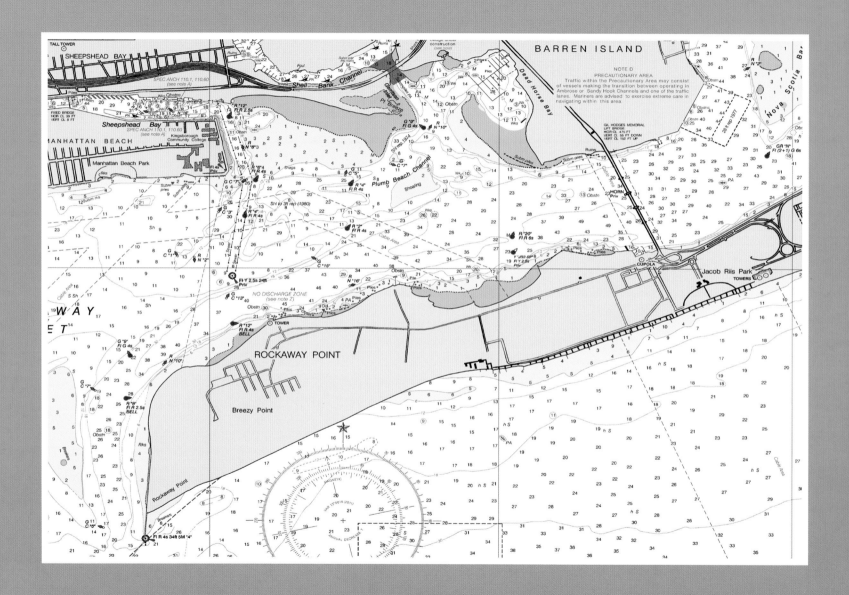

I'd looked forward to this outing for several days. Now the weather had put a stop to it. But sitting below deck with nowhere to go and a steaming cup of coffee in front of me, I wasn't utterly disappointed. Rather, I had an overwhelming feeling of freedom. My schedule for the day suddenly opened up. Besides, there were always plenty of things to do on a boat. Winches needed to be lubricated, lines spliced, blocks adjusted, the engine's oil changed and the sealing on the leaking starboard bulkhead replaced. The list went on, but looking across the misty bay, I felt the urge to explore a part of the Rockaway shoreline on which I had not spent much time. I'd sailed along its coast from Jacob Riis Park to the tip of Breezy Point many times, and during these journeys I'd seen some of the houses and armories of the old, abandoned Fort Tilden from afar. Now I was curious to take a closer look. Some of the buildings from the old Rockaway Naval Air Station were still standing. This was where the Curtiss seaplane NC-4, known as the flying boat, took off for her first transatlantic passage in 1919. That flight wrote as much aviation history as Lindbergh's first non-stop Atlantic crossing ten years later, taking off from Roosevelt field on Long Island.

Today the best way to get to Fort Tilden beach is by foot through the parking lot of Jacob Riis Park, and after only a few minutes I found myself walking through the grand entrance of the park between two art deco bathhouses built in a half circle. On the right side of the entrance stood a bust of the man for whom the park was named. Jacob Riis, a Danish-born photographer, exposed New York's slums to the world at the end of the nineteenth century. Forty years later, Robert Moses designed the park as a refuge for the poor living in the same cramped tenements on Manhattan's Lower East Side, or along the avenues in Brooklyn, and it has been known as "the people's beach" ever since.

The beautiful bathhouses have been closed for years because of asbestos pollution. Recently the National Park Administration spent twenty million dollars to clean the buildings, but that left no money for renovation. Now nothing but the restroom area and a small section for concession stands are open to the public, and only during the summer. On this early October day, all the buildings were boarded up with plywood and the place looked utterly abandoned.

The sprawling beach is 150 feet wide from the promenade to the sea, and with the low-hanging fog, the horizon line merged with the breaking waves. It's a four-mile hike to Rockaway Point, and other than the Silver Gull Beach Club, about halfway to the western tip of the peninsula, there are no buildings visible on the waterfront.

Walking along the dunes, I looked at some of the structures that once belonged to Fort Tilden. A dense and lush forest vegetation had overtaken the old Nike missile stations constructed during the Cold War, its nuclear weapons designed to deter attacking Soviet warplanes while they were still far out over the ocean—a scenario that luckily never happened. Decommissioned after Richard Nixon and Leonid Brezhnev signed the Anti-Ballistic Missile Treaty in 1972, this fort was simply left to nature. The military slammed the doors and handed the National Park Administration the keys. Not much has changed since then. A few hundred yards southwest of the official beach area, the coastline looked almost untouched. No paved walkways or boardwalks or lifeguards. This makes swimming there technically illegal, which in turn attracts a crowd that doesn't want to mix with families and screaming kids and ice cream trucks and food vendors in the overcrowded section of the shore.

After a few days of rain and strong fall winds, driftwood, tree branches, old beams, plastic bottles, food containers, and all sorts of flotsam littered the beach. Someone had made a few abstract sculptures out of the garbage. Facing the sea with nothing to do, people become creative. Figures fashioned out of tree branches were adorned with shells that hung like primitive Christmas ornaments or the visions of a spiritual dreamer.

The tide was still low and the receding sea carved little creeks into the sand that I now had to wade through. The water was warm and soothing, but I had to pay attention to the time. With the tide coming in, I might have to walk back through the dunes and I wasn't sure how accessible the area was. The fog hugged the landscape like a soft, low-hanging cloud, forming tiny droplets that made each reed blade shine like a shard of well-polished steel.

The fog hugged the landscape like a soft, low-hanging cloud, forming tiny droplets that made each reed blade shine like a shard of well-polished steel.

The seascape looked as if all the color had been sucked out of it, a monochrome scale of gray and beige, a color scheme of sorrow and sadness. Seagulls on the rocks, disturbed by my presence, screamed and took off into the clouds. My eyes scanned the sea, thinking of the many ships that had been lost there over the centuries. Who could imagine that at the entrance of one of the most famous harbors in the world, more shipwrecks rested in the sandy bottom per square mile than at any other place in the world? Skippers from all around the globe call this tranquil place Wreck Valley. Even today ships regularly run aground or sink just off the coast of Rockaway.

June 6, 1993, was one of these tragic days. Ten people died when the cargo ship *Golden Venture* got stranded in heavy weather. On board were 286 refugees from China, who had each paid tens of thousands of dollars for the two-month journey to freedom, crammed into containers with too little food and water. Hitting a heavy storm on the Atlantic, the ship barely made it into New York waters. When small rendezvous boats failed to show up to ferry the illegal passengers to shore, the Indonesian captain tried to take the vessel into harbor, but the Chinese smugglers, afraid of capture, confined him to his cabin. The vessel, out of control, ran aground. Only 300 feet from shore, many of the immigrants, fearing deportation, jumped into the water and swam for it. But exhausted from the long journey, and fighting a strong current, ten never made it. They drowned right there. Those who survived were detained, and many spent as long as three years in jail. In the end, 111 were deported back to China, and thirty-five received political asylum. The rest are still in the country, without any legal status whatsoever.

I walked on. I wanted to make it all the way to the western point of the peninsula, but when I came to the Silver Gull Beach Club, the water had already risen to the lower cabins and there was no way to pass, so I turned around and started my walk back to the boat.

The seascape looked as if all the color had been sucked out of it, a monochrome scale of gray and beige,
a color scheme of sorrow and sadness.

40°34.38'N - 074°03.12'W

AT SEA IN THE CITY

The north by northwest wind had significantly freshened up to twenty miles per hour. I was sailing upwind and the boat was heeling at thirty degrees, running almost seven knots. If the wind increased further, I would have to reef the genoa to take the pressure off the rudder. But for now, everything was near-perfect. I was heading in the direction of two man-made islands in New York's lower bay, Swinburne and Hoffman.

Looking at the telltales of the genoa, I made sure both stayed in an optimal streaming position, slightly adjusting the wheel every so often. This was sailing at its best: the sheets perfectly trimmed, the water calm, and the wind steady. Still, I had to stay focused. Falling off even a little or luffing a bit too hard would have stayed the boat's speed. The point was to stay in sync with the forces of nature. That's what sailing is all about.

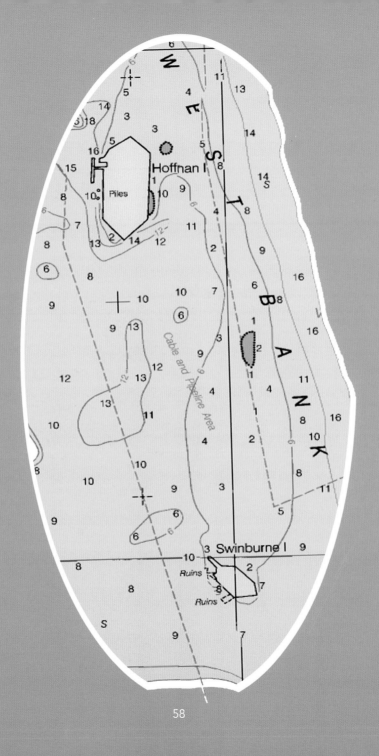

Given the effortless movement of the boat, it would take less than an hour to leave Coney Island and Seagate, a private, gated community northwest of the amusement parks, behind. I was aiming for the southern edge of Swinburne, planning to tack there and turn northeast toward Fort Hamilton on the east side of the Verrazano-Narrows Bridge. From there I would make my way into New York Harbor, pass Staten Island on the port side, and head toward Governors Island with Liberty and Ellis Islands to the west—a short sail that would take me across six islands, including Long Island behind me, before I reached the seventh, Manhattan.

Swinburne and Hoffman were soon right ahead of me, and I already could make out the ruins on the more southerly and smaller of the two, Swinburne, named after the city's health commissioner in the 1870s, when both islands were constructed from landfill. Hoffman was named after the mayor and future governor.

Both islands were part of the early US immigration system. Before Ellis Island, the gateway to America, opened in 1890, these islands housed a quarantine station and a hospital for infectious diseases. At the time, inspectors would board the immigrant-laden ships even before they reached Manhattan and order off anybody with symptoms of yellow fever or other contagious illnesses. The sick would then be brought to the hospital on Swinburne or held in quarantine on Hoffman. A young woman from Staten Island, Alice Austen, regarded as the first professional female photographer in America, documented the islands for ten years, beginning in 1890. Later in the day, I would catch sight of her house on the eastern shore of Staten Island, now a museum where her images can be seen.

Approaching Swinburne, I thought of how it was Bill Kornblum's book that first inspired me to buy a boat and start sailing around New York. I came to the Big Apple from Europe in the early 1990s, and to me the neglected waterfront in Manhattan and Brooklyn was almost incomprehensible. In Europe, waterfront real estate is always the most desirable, and its promenade, cafés, and restaurants are the most popular places in town. In New York, on the other hand, nobody seemed to care. On Manhattan's west side, dilapidated docks made it dangerous to get close to the water, and the old, decaying warehouses of South Brooklyn looked like gigantic movie sets for underground horror films.

All of this only inflamed my desire to find an apartment near the water or, even better, to find a boat and sail it. But there was no place to rent one, and owning a boat in New York seemed far-fetched. On occasional trips to Coney Island or Manhattan Beach I would see sailboats passing, but I had no idea where they were coming from. Then, one day in the early 2000s, I spotted a book called *At Sea in the City* whose cover photograph showed a boat with a red sail gliding in front of the Manhattan skyline.

The book told the story of a sociology professor in New York, William Kornblum, who bought and restored a hundred-year-old catboat while raising a family, and he sailed it from island to island throughout the metropolitan area. His story settled it: My dream could actually happen. Sure, it took another few years before I finally wrote the check for my very own sloop, but along the way I met William Kornblum himself, a tall intellectual who invited me onto his boat. "Call me Bill" he said, while I was boarding his working boat with one main sail of the type used by fishermen around Cape Cod for hundreds of years.

Bill's approach to sailing immediately resonated with me. For him, sailing was about reliving history, connecting with the origin of a place. We stayed in touch. Finally, when I had *Sojourn*, I invited Bill to sail with me. When we passed Swinburne and Hoffman, he observed how the water in New York connects and separates everything at the same time. Over the centuries, the islands of New York had been used to divide New Yorkers. The rich and healthy lived in Manhattan, the poor worked the docks of Brooklyn, the sick were interned on Swinburne, Hoffmann, or North Brother Island, the mentally ill housed in the psychiatric wards of Welfare (today Roosevelt) Island, criminals incarcerated on Rikers Island, and the unknown dead buried on the country's largest potter field on Hart Island; different worlds telling innumerable stories, all connected by water.

THROUGH HELL AND INTO
THE SOUND

Winds blowing from the west at ten to twelve miles per hour filled both sails. The boat cut steadily through the calm water and the meter showed a speed of four-and-a-half knots. I was in the middle of the Ambrose Channel, about half a mile from the Verrazano-Narrows Bridge. An enormous cargo ship was coming toward me, carrying more than 5,000 containers. It was close enough for me to read the name, *MSC Bremen*, a town in my native Germany, painted in big letters on the bow, but still far enough for me to safely cross the channel toward Brooklyn. Or so I thought.

I leaned back, enjoying the warm spring breeze, when suddenly the booming horn of the approaching cargo ship startled me out of my daydreaming. Scanning the water and shoreline around me, I realized my position had hardly changed and the 60,000-ton freighter was dangerously close. I jumped to my feet and clung to the wheel. What was going on? I turned on the GPS, and a split-second later a beep confirmed that the device had acquired a satellite signal. The captain of the fast-approaching cargo ship blew his horn rapidly in five short bursts, making clear that I was in immediate danger of collision. The vessel still seemed reasonably far off, but it is difficult to estimate the speed of those giant carriers.

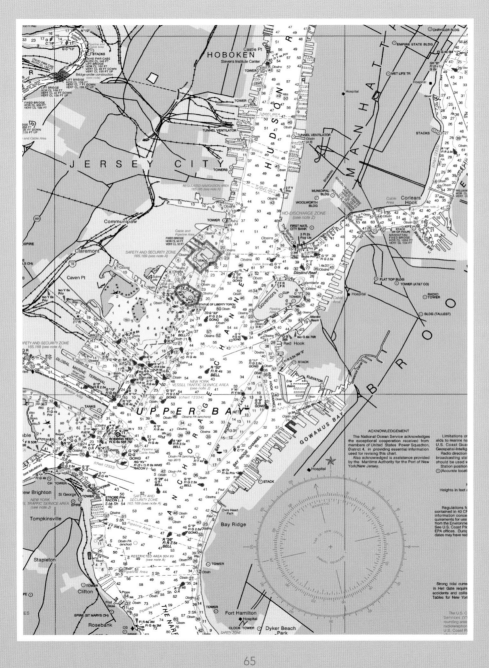

From the corner of my eye I caught the speed gauge on the GPS: 0.5 knots. The boat's knot meter, meanwhile, still showed a steady 4.5. I had made a major mistake. I remembered the different ways to gauge a boat's speed. The knot meter measured how fast it moved through the water and the GPS its pace over ground. Because of the current, a boat can easily cut through the water at four knots while moving at just one knot from point A to point B. In this way, it is easy to think you're moving forward when you're not.

I cursed like an old sea bear and immediately started the engine, slamming it into gear and pushing it to full throttle, the sails flapping as I got out of the leviathan's way. A minute later, the container ship passed on my port side. Some of the deckhands waved hello.

This happened when I was a rookie sailor on my maiden trip to Manhattan. But today, years later, on an equally beautiful spring day, I had done everything right, planning the trip out carefully and taking into consideration the Atlantic Coast tides.

I was on my way into the Long Island Sound and crossing the lower bay into the New York Harbor, an estuary where several rivers meet the sea and produce strong currents. The Hudson, the largest of them, changes its direction every six hours and so does the East River. In spite of its name, the latter is not a stream but a tidal strait that at times flows in the opposite direction to the Hudson. Conflicting currents often make the water look like it is boiling, and sometimes, even with a strong wind, a sailboat leans heavily but is not moving forward at all. To maneuver these waters with a small craft like *Sojourn* I had to take the tidal forces into account, especially when passing one of the most dangerous straits on the Eastern Seaboard, Hell Gate in the East River.

Today, there are detailed tidal charts and it is easy to use a favorable current for the voyage. I had left the Gateway Marina an hour after low tide at the Battery, and two-and-a-half hours later I was approaching the Verrazano-Narrows Bridge.

Looking up at its 228-foot clearance, it seemed to shrink my boat to the size of a tiny nutshell, while the *Queen Mary II* that sometimes docks on the Brooklyn shore just barely clears the bridge. With Staten Island on the port side and Bay Ridge, Brooklyn, on starboard, I was sailing into the mouth of the natural New York Harbor, a group of islands on its own.

I still couldn't see the tip of Manhattan. The coastline of New Jersey, Liberty Island, and even part of Governors Island blended together on the horizon. Just before reaching the American Veterans Memorial Pier that extends Bay Ridge Avenue into the Upper Bay, the Manhattan skyscrapers came into sight. Moving along the line that separates New York and New Jersey in the middle of the harbor, the iconic city looked astonishingly small and manageable. The image of the new World Trade Center, always connected with the burned-in memory of watching the Twin Towers collapse from my kitchen window in Brooklyn, left me wistful. On that painful September day, my relationship to the city changed, gaining an intimacy nurtured by the vulnerability of a hurt soul.

There were not many boats in the harbor at this early hour, only busy ferries shuttling people between the islands, creating choppy waves in the harbor. But the wind was good in my sail and the current was in my favor. I was cutting right through, passing the Lehigh Valley Barge of the waterfront museum, and soon I made a sharp turn to starboard to enter the small Buttermilk Channel between Brooklyn and Governors Island. It isn't clear how this body of water got its name. One tale says that Brooklyn dairy farmers used to ferry their products to market in Manhattan and the rough water would churn them into buttermilk. Not very convincing, but neither is the explanation that the poet Walt Whitman had to offer. In an article about the history of Brooklyn, he reported that the strait between Brooklyn and Governors Island at low tide was so shallow that the farmers drove their cattle right through it to the pastures on Governors Island. However, nautical maps dating back to the 1700s tell a different story.

The image of the new World Trade Center, always connected with the burned-in memory of watching the Twin Towers collapse from my kitchen window in Brooklyn, left me wistful.

Before entering the East River, I decided to take in the sails. Being alone on the boat, I had more control when under motor, and I didn't want to get in the way of the fast East River ferries. As soon as I had fastened the main to the boom, I turned around and started up the East River, passing South Street Seaport and sailing under the Brooklyn Bridge. I was making six to seven knots even though I was running the engine at less than half throttle, a clear sign that the current had changed and the river was flowing east.

The water appeared pretty smooth at first, but then the bow lifted itself violently out of the water and slammed down hard after each wave. There were swirls of water left and right. It didn't take much imagination to envision the small boat going out of control. I heard the crash of some things falling in the cabin. Worst of all, I had forgotten to close the front hatch, and with each wave water was gushing onto my bunk.

I approached Roosevelt Island with Belmont Island on my starboard side. Belmont isn't really an island, but a by-product of the construction of the Steinway Tunnel under the East River. In 1891, when the German piano manufacturer wanted to connect his factory in Queens with Manhattan, he partnered with railroad entrepreneur August Belmont Jr. to build the tunnel. Today, the New York subway's 7 line runs through it. The man-made island came to fame in 2004, when artist and filmmaker Duke Riley occupied it during the Republican National Convention, raising a flag and declaring the island a sovereign nation. His occupancy and the newly founded nation didn't last long. A Coast Guard boat equipped with machine guns swiftly apprehended the artist. Riley, the first artist to have explored the unknown islands of New York as part of his work, once created a speakeasy bar underneath a bridge of the Bell Parkway right off Dead Horse Bay, and another time piloted a self-made submarine to approach the *Queen Mary II.*

I was now running at nine knots and hadn't even reached Hell Gate. I had almost passed Roosevelt and was approaching Mill Rock, another small, uninhabited island in the East River south of Randall's Island, which was now lying in front of me. Above me loomed the Triborough Bridge (now called Robert F. Kennedy Bridge) and the I-278, the Bronx-Queens Expressway that crosses Randall's Island into Manhattan. By way of this highway, millions of people come onto Randall's Island without even knowing it exists.

The waters are wild, here where the East River and the Harlem River split. I was right in Hell Gate, and the water boiled under the Hell Gate Railroad Bridge. *Sojourn* was pushed through Hell Gate, making more than ten knots. Until the mid-1800s the wild tidal waters had forced hundreds, if not thousands, of ships onto the rocks of Hell Gate and smashed them to pieces.

In 1851, the Army Corps of Engineers began to blow up the treacherous underwater obstacles and created a navigable channel, a process that would take more than seventy years. The largest explosion came from about 300,000 pounds of dynamite and caused a waterspout 250 feet high. But although the rocks were destroyed, Hell Gate remains a difficult water to navigate for a small vessel like mine. Trying to sail against its strong current by relying on a thirty-five-year-old, sixteen-horsepower diesel engine would probably just kill the motor.

I was following the course of Dutch sailor Adriaen Block, who in 1614 became the first European to sail up the East River into the Sound. He had named the tidal strait that he encountered on the way Hellegate, sometimes translated by some as "the Hole of Hell," while others argued that the word *helle* could also mean bright, describing a beautiful place for fishing and hunting. Given the danger the place has posed to vessels for centuries, for me calling it Hell made perfect sense.

Block and his crew were the first known Europeans to settle on the island of Manhattan after their ship *Tiger* was destroyed in a fire. Although there is no reliable record, it is said that he lived peacefully for at least three years with the natives that populated Mannahatta. Here he and his crew built a new ship, the forty-four-foot *Onrust,* known to the English as *Restless*, which he used to explore the Long Island Sound. During his journeys, Block created the first accurate East Coast map from New York to Cape Cod, showing Long Island disconnected from the mainland, and naming the New York area an *archipelagus*.

I had hardly cleared the bridge when the water calmed down, the boat slowed, and I passed another pair of islands: North Brother and its twin South Brother. I was well on my way into the Long Island Sound.

40°51.77'N - 073°46.80'N
LOST TREASURES OF
THE SOUND

I had passed Hell Gate uneventfully. The twin islands, North and South Brother, lay behind me, and so did Rikers, New York's prison island in the East River. Though it was only 10:30 in the morning, it felt much later. I had started the day's journey at the crack of dawn, around 4:30 a.m. and almost twenty miles away. For the last three hours, the New York skyline had moved past my eyes in one constant stream, like a film in slow motion, and the rising sun had lit the scenery perfectly. Sailing under the Hell Gate Bridge with the boat pushed by a strong easterly current to a speed of ten knots was like riding a roller coaster on the water.

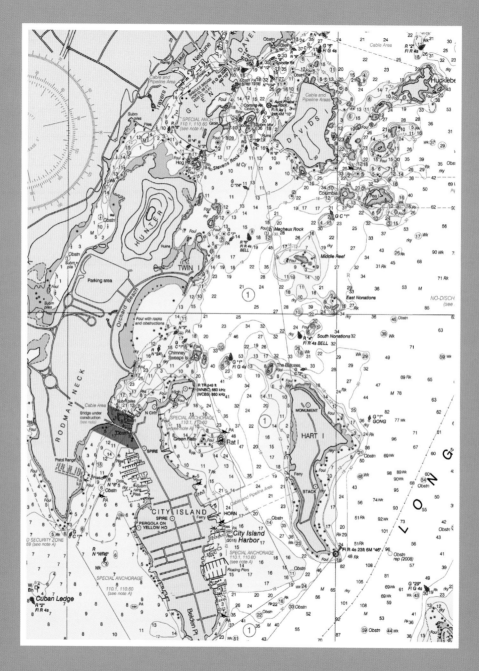

At Hunts Point, where the Bronx River connects with the East River, the stream was calm and the monotone rhythm of the diesel engine created an almost tranquil atmosphere. The wind hadn't woken up yet and there was no point in setting sail. After the excitement of sailing up the East River and passing Hell Gate, it was time for a break. The shore between the Whitestone and the Throgs Neck Bridge differed starkly from the buzzing early-morning traffic on FDR Drive on Manhattan's East side parallel to the river. After passing the industrial buildings around La Guardia Airport, the first waterfront houses of the Long Island Sound, with boat docks connected to the lawns, came into sight.

Entering the Sound after clearing the Throgs Neck Bridge, I turned to portside and was cruising along the 1.2 miles of the west side of City Island under motor.

Hundreds of sailboats of all sizes bobbed on their moorings around City Island, only thirty minutes by car from Manhattan. They belonged to nine marinas and eight yacht clubs, remnants of a nautical history that made the island famous as the home of the America's Cup teams' most winning yachts. This is where they were built and maintained, and it is still the place in New York City where one can find the best boat mechanics and sail makers.

For the last three hours, the New York skyline had moved past my eyes in one constant stream,
like a film in slow motion.

City Islanders are a breed of their own. Only 4,000 people live here, and hardly ever does a stranger settle in one of the old wooden houses that once were home to boat builders and fishermen. One of the few outsiders who chose to live in this tightly knit community was the famous neurologist and writer, Oliver Sacks. In a little shack on the shore of City Island he wrote *Awakenings*, a story about his work at the Beth Abraham Hospital's chronic care facility in the Bronx that became an Oscar-nominated blockbuster movie, starring Robert De Niro and Robin Williams. Sacks was fascinated by the remoteness of islands and what that does to its inhabitants. He wrote: "Islands are experiments of nature, places blessed or cursed by geographic singularity to harbor unique forms of life," an observation that very much inspired me to explore the island world of New York and the people who live there.

I was deep in thought about this when I suddenly saw a Swiss flag flying side-by-side with an American flag on a speck of land between the Bronx and Hart Island. Two Swiss-American businessmen had bought uninhabited Rat Island in 2011, which had once been home to New York's smallest artist colony. For a long time it was one of the few privately owned islands in New York. Rat Island really isn't much more than a tiny speck of land in the water, and the two men only bought the land to make sure that no one else would build on it and obstruct the view from their City Island house. A few miles east, another New Yorker is living out his Robinson Crusoe fantasy. He bought Columbia Island, also known as Little Pea, that once served TV broadcaster CBS as a transmitter station. The new owner wants to transform what's left of the old structures into a self-sufficient green home.

I was heading toward Pelham Bay and the white sand of Orchard Beach on Hunter and Twin Islands, which are now connected to the mainland. The only beach in the Bronx was man-made, with sand brought in from the Rockaway peninsula. When the park was completed in the 1930s, the people of the Bronx called it "the Riviera of New York."

With hardly any wind in the sails, I slowly moved east through another treacherous waterway surrounding the big city. From Eastchester Bay to Portchester, at the border to Connecticut, the sea is dotted with two dozen islands with names like Huckleberry, Goose, and David, whose rocky shores form little bays that look like Norwegian fjords, where seals live during the winter months.

For centuries, those little islands were perfect hideouts for the pirates who controlled the Long Island Sound, avoiding British taxes and smuggling goods into Manhattan. In 1695, the British admiralty and Lord Bellomont, the governor of New York, appointed a wealthy Scottish privateer, Captain William Kidd, to protect British ships from piracy. Bellomont and his friends raised the money to furnish a ship for Captain Kidd, an investment that should have brought them enormous profits by entitling them to keep a large portion of the booty. But for more than a year, Captain Kidd had no luck hunting pirates. His crew, sailing under the common "no loot, no pay" agreement, was broke and ready to mutiny. According to the tale, Captain Kidd eventually turned into a pirate himself, and his former business partner, Lord Bellomont, commanded by King William III, made out an arrest warrant for the once-honorable businessman from lower Manhattan. Kidd, intending to clear his name, sailed back to New York, and entered the archipelago through the Long Island Sound in 1699. On his way to Manhattan, he stopped on several islands. First on Gardiners Island, east of Long Island, and later on one of the little ones now spread out in front of me. One of them is believed to be the island where he hid his stolen treasure. Many continue to believe it to this day, but as yet not a single silver coin has turned up.

40°58.43'N - 073°33.10'W

TIME IS GAUGED BY THE CHANGE OF LIGHT

Climbing on deck at four a.m., the night enveloped me in monochrome shades of blue, meshing together water and sky. I felt alone. At that eerily quiet hour, with a shimmer of light on the horizon, even the birds were still asleep.

I untied the lines, turned on the motor and, as quietly as I could, moved slowly through the calm water, heading east toward where the sun would soon rise over the Long Island Sound.

In the middle of the Sound I cut the engine and let the boat float. I sat on the foredeck and watched the light change. Soon the rising sun's red glow turned everything strawberry-milk pink, then, a few minutes later, orange yellow. For twenty minutes the sun burned through the low clouds and cleared the sky.

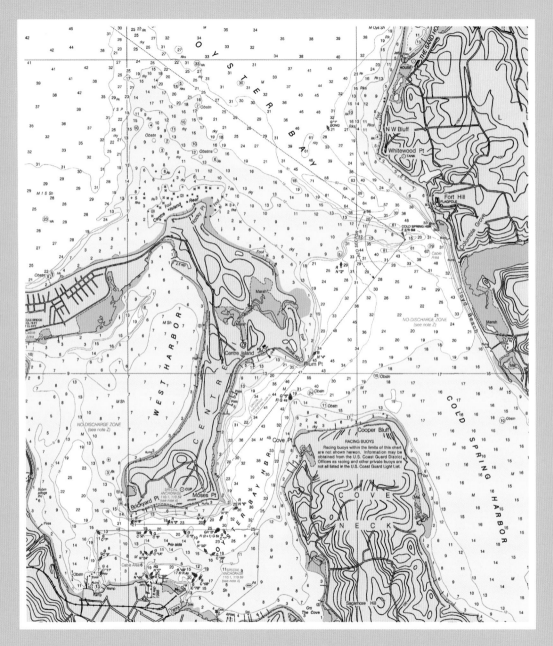

Before the British carpenter John Harrison built the first seaworthy chronograph in 1750, the time of the day was often determined by the course of the sun, and experienced seafarers could tell the hour by looking at the color of the sky. For them, time was not a commodity but the quintessential information needed to define their exact position. Sailors could gauge their latitude through celestial observations, but they needed to know the exact time of the day at zero-degree longitude, or what is called a prime meridian, to calculate the second coordinate of their location.

For endless generations of sailors, observing nature and dead reckoning—the process of assessing a ship's location through constantly recording its course and speed—was essential in plotting a route. Today, with cell phones and tablets offering exact geographic information on demand, it is surprising to realize that the GPS has only been available to mariners for the last few decades. But as useful as the GPS is, watching a New York cab driver turn one on when asked to drive to the corner of 39th Street and 11th Avenue warns me that there is a dangerous downside to the technology: the loss of a sense of place, the unconscious knowledge of where one is.

Many animals move back and forth from one place to another without any maps or instruments. They are guided by the sun, the magnetic fields of the Earth, by sounds, or even odors. Unconscious about what leads them, an instinctive sense of place is essential for their survival.

Being on the water with no land in sight, it occurs to me that humans, too, must have had the ability to sense their whereabouts and to feel in which direction they were moving. Long before Columbus and all the other known explorers, thousands of years ago, humans crossed the world's oceans, knowing very little about the stars or the course of the sun.

Being on the water with no land in sight, it occurs to me that humans, too, must have had the ability to sense their whereabouts and to feel in which direction they were moving.

I closed my eyes and lay on my back on the foredeck. The boat slowly rode the current of the Sound. No engine, no sails set. The boat moved in one direction and I tried to feel which. With no land reference, and no sun, it was impossible. I thought with envy about the sailors of the Marshall Islands in the Pacific who'd mastered the art of wave piloting, the ability to read the waves with their bodies to learn direction and tell how far they were from land. This ancient art passed from one sailor to the next, but was kept secret from others. Scientists believe that this ability to read nature's clues to gain a sense of place guided humans for millennia, but vanished with the discovery of celestial navigation.

The Marshall Island sailors were the only exception, capable of navigating without maps or instruments in modern times. Following the US hydrogen bomb tests in the 1950s, most of the islands became uninhabitable and the people, with their unique skill for navigation, disappeared. Analyzing their DNA, scientists have since found more proof of their navigational mastership: they were the descendants of humans in Southeast Asia, 4,000 miles away from the Marshall Islands.

With the wind picking up, the *Sojourn* gathered speed. I was still lying with my eyes closed on the foredeck, but I could sense it. No sails were set; it could have only been a small increase, but by consciously focusing I could actually *feel* us moving forward.

I thought with envy about the sailors of the Marshall Islands in the Pacific who'd mastered the art of wave piloting, the ability to read the waves with their bodies to learn direction and tell how far they were from land.

ORIENT BY THE SEA

Oyster Bay lay behind me. I carefully maneuvered out of the harbor, a vast mooring field with hundreds of fishing boats and sailing vessels swinging around white balls. Center Island lay on the port side. It was the fifth of July. The previous night I'd been aboard the *Sojourn* celebrating Independence Day, watching the fireworks, when I noticed dozens of sky lanterns lifting off from Center Island into the dark midsummer night. Today, while taking on fuel, the dock master told me that the famous musician Billy Joel, who owns a house on this secluded peninsula, had celebrated his wedding.

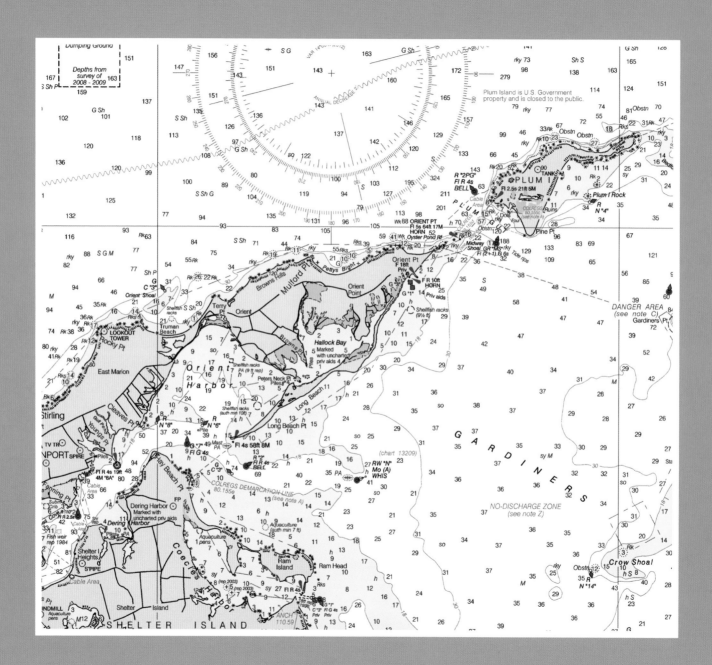

Pulling out toward Rocky Point, a half-dozen fishing boats and bay men searching for clams joined me on the water. Then, as I was entering the Long Island Sound heading toward the Connecticut shore, I turned around at the helm and looked back at the North Shore of Long Island. This area is also known as the Gold Coast, because the lavish mansions of the Vanderbilts, Whitneys, and Morgans, who had made their fortunes during the first industrial revolution, dot the cliffs of Oyster Bay, Huntington, and West Neck, often only seen from the water. Built in the early twentieth century, during New York's Gilded Age, when money from the railroad and oil boom financed more than 500 such sprawling estates, these mansions were often protected from the common man by high walls, behind which the rich and famous of Scott Fitzgerald's *The Great Gatsby* were hard at play.

But the days when magnificent yachts anchored in the Northport Bay are long gone, wiped out by the Great Depression, when many of the once-glamorous mansions fell into disrepair. Today only a few are left, like the Vanderbilt Mansion, now a museum that provides a glimpse into the era of the tycoons.

Leaving the Gold Coast behind, I passed Port Jefferson. From there to Orient Point, Long Island's easternmost tip at North Fork, cliffs and rocky shores stretch for more than forty miles with no safe harbor but the inlet of Mattituck about halfway to the east. I had no reason to stop there this time, and I was keen on getting from Oyster Bay to Orient in one leg during this trip. Depending on the wind, it can be quite a long day of sailing. Good timing was the most important factor for a smooth voyage. Piloting the Long Island Sound requires taking different currents at different times into consideration. On my way east I took advantage of the ebbing tide, whose strength is caused by The Race, a two- to four-mile opening to the Atlantic between Fishers Island and Plum Island east of Orient Point. There, the water's depth plunges to more than 250 feet, creating a strong siphoning effect on the entire eastern part of the Sound. During ebb at The Race, a constant current of one to one-and-a-half knots flows east. I planned to take advantage of this natural force to arrive at Orient Point at slack tide, the short period between flood and ebb. From there, I wanted to sail through Plum Gut, a very narrow channel between Orient Point and Plum Island, into Gardiners Bay, which was marked by a lighthouse called the Coffee Pot.

Crisscrossing the Sound between Connecticut and northern Long Island, I headed toward Branford Harbor. I looked carefully at the chart while approaching the Connecticut shore to avoid the shallow water and the rocks that make it dangerous. And there they were, right in front of me, the mussel-overgrown boulders that are evidence of Connecticut and Long Island's racially charged history: Until 1836, these rocks appeared as "Nigger Heads" in the charts. By 1855, they were re-named to Negro Heads, and it took seventy years until the Connecticut State Senate took up an initiative in 2015 to change the name once again. However, this turned out not to be an easy endeavor. Finally an essay competition among Connecticut high school students brought a solution. The lucky winner, Kelly Tiernan from Branford High, suggested renaming the boulders Sowheag Rocks, remembering the leader of the Native American Wangunks tribe who sold most of their land to the new colony of Connecticut around 1637. The new name will be submitted to the US Board on Geographic Names for a final decision.

I tacked and turned back toward the North Shore. A good dozen commercial fishing boats were on the water. The hard lives of fishermen and bay men hasn't changed much over the last decades, but their numbers have dwindled. The few left struggle with outdated federal catch quotas that were once meant to protect overfished species such as fluke and sea bass, but do not acknowledge that since then, the Sound's water temperature has risen by five degrees and improved the habitat of these species. Bound by the law, commercial fishermen are forced to throw a big portion of their valuable haul back into the water. The fish, caught during the hard day's work, are often already dead.

Work and play go hand-in-hand in the eastern part of the Long Island Sound: The few remaining commercial fishermen are joined by hundreds of recreational boaters who fish the waters of the Sound. Small marinas like Orient by the Sea, facing Gardiner's Bay, offer boats for hire for fishing trips into the bay. That's where I was headed.

Sailing around the Coffee Pot lighthouse at the tip of Long Island, the water literally boiled, jerking the boat back and forth, the swirls capped by white foam that make the sheer force of the currents visible to the naked eye. Under full sail I had turned the motor on to ensure additional navigation support, particularly important because the ferry that connects Long Island to Connecticut frequents this channel, too.

The hard lives of fishermen and bay men hasn't changed much over the last decades,
but their numbers have dwindled.

The marina Orient by the Sea sits next to the ferry terminal with a bottleneck entry channel marked by wooden pilings and buoys. The water near the shore is shallow and, for a sailboat with almost five feet of draft, staying within the channel is essential. Entering the little marina, I noticed that no other sailboat had tied up at the docks. I was excited to spend the night at this place. The harbormaster assigned the dock closest to the narrow entrance channel where I tied up. I enjoyed a cold beer at the outdoor bar. Potted palm trees and the fishermen talking about their catch of the day gave this place a Hemingway aura. Tired from a long day of sailing, I soon was deep asleep in my berth. When I woke up in the morning and stepped out on the dock, I realized why no other sailboat was here. At low tide, my keel was stuck in the mud.

A dense fog was hovering over Gardiners Bay. Standing on the break wall, I could hear the foghorns of the nearby ferry that was nowhere to be seen. Imagining how terrifying it can be on the water, with nothing in sight! I was happy to stay until the water had risen and the fog lifted.

Imagining how terrifying it can be on the water, with nothing in sight!
I was happy to stay until the water had risen and the fog lifted.

41°05.29'N - 072°08.35'W
THE FIRST LADY OF GARDINERS ISLAND

With the wind blowing directly from the west, I sailed downwind from Greenport Harbor along the Long Beach Bar into Gardiners Bay. The main sail was out on the port side and the genoa on starboard. I was sailing *wing on wing . . . a butterfly without a whisker pole*, which meant I had to make sure to keep the boat in a perfect downwind position for the genoa not to fold. The Long Beach Bar Lighthouse, locally known as the "Bug Lighthouse," a Victorian structure, was originally built on wooden piles in 1870, which made the building look like a giant water bug at low tide. It burned to the ground on July 4, 1963, and the beacon was rebuilt in the 1990s.

Heading to Montauk Point on the eastern tip of Long Island's South Fork, I sailed by Gardiners Island, which sits in the Long Island Sound like a lotus flower in a pond. Beautiful and almost untouched, Gardiners is the largest privately owned island in the US, and the only real estate still owned by the same family to whom the king of England had given it. With the blessing of Charles I, Lion Gardiner bought the island from the Montaukett tribe in 1639, and to this day the six-mile-long, three-mile-wide island is off limits to the general public. There are only two buildings: Gardiner's main house and the white windmill on its west side. But although the island was hardly populated, it became the site of a witchcraft trial thirty-five years before the Salem trials of 1692, when Gardiner's daughter died after reportedly seeing a witch.

Almost 200 years later, another and luckier Gardiner descendent came to a different fame. Julia Gardiner moved straight from the island into the White House in 1844 when she became the second wife of President John Tyler and the First Lady of the United States.

Northwest from me and opposite Gardiners Island, I could make out the shoreline of Plum Island with the lighthouse on its west end. Thomas Harris calls it Anthrax Island in *Silence of the Lambs,* recommending it as a vacation spot for the psychopathological killer Hannibal Lecter.

Called *Manittuwond* by the Pequot, the island was bought by Europeans settlers in 1659. It then passed through twenty-two different owners before the US government finally bought it to expand Fort Terry in 1899; and it was here that in 1952 the army established its infamous Lab 257. A research institute for biological weapons shrouded in secrecy, the remote island laboratory set people's imaginations aflame. It didn't help that it was run by a high-ranking former Nazi, Erich Traub, brought to the US after WWII as part of Operation Paperclip, a

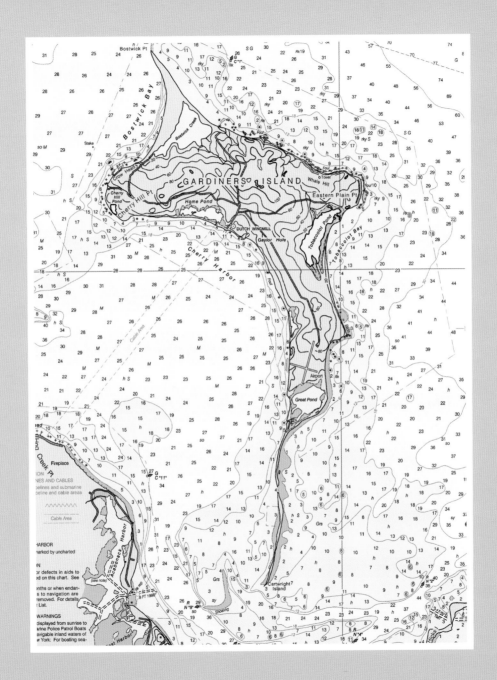

program to recruit scientists from defeated Germany. A virologist, Traub led experiments with a wide range of viruses designed to destroy an enemy's food supply. And when the deformed bodies of weird animals began to wash ashore on Montauk, rumors worthy of the best science fiction began to circulate. But nothing was ever proven, and the research was short-lived. In 1954, the US Department of Agriculture took over the Plum Island labs and began work developing a vaccination to protect American livestock from foot and mouth disease.

Sailing along these islands and taking a close look at the nautical charts, it wasn't hard to imagine how it might have been back when this area was the first line of defense against an attack on New York City, a hundred miles to the west. Indeed, in 1942 a German submarine entered the Long Island Sound carrying eight Nazi terrorists on a secret sabotage mission. Detected by the Coast Guard, the sub was forced to surface and the Germans were arrested. Rather than trying the Nazis in a civil court under the rules of due process, President Roosevelt instead decided to set up a secret military tribunal, which eventually sentenced the invaders to death. Sixty years later, this case became the precedent for President George W. Bush's secret military courts for non-combatant enemies in the aftermath of 9/11, and eventually led to the opening of the prison on Guantanamo Bay.

Unintentionally, my sailing to the tip of Long Island had become a journey into US military history—and it didn't stop when Plum Island was out of sight. The next landmark was Montauk Lighthouse, atop the Montauk cliffs with a group of buildings with gigantic parabolic antennas nearby. Long since decommissioned, the complex once belonged to another defense project, one intended to detect approaching ships more than 200 miles out at sea. When satellite technology made the enormous structures void, the military planned to tear the antennas down, but the Montauk fishermen objected; they were better landmarks than the 110-foot-high Montauk Point Light, erected in 1797.

Those strangely futuristic antennas from the past were now my landmarks, too. I was still sailing downwind on a beautiful day. Though both sails were now on the starboard side, there had been hardly anything to do on this short journey. Soon I could make out the entrance to Lake Montauk, a freshwater lake until 1929, when a Miami developer who dreamed of turning Montauk into South Beach decided to blast away the land separating the lake from the ocean. The wind freshened up a bit, and I entered the harbor under full sail. Colorful and rusty fishing trawlers lined the docks alongside modern white recreational fishing boats of every size. Though this is still a major base for the US Coast Guard, the military was nowhere to be seen.

41°15.90'N - 072°00.44'W

THE PRINCE'S ISLAND

On my way to Fishers Island I had sailed beyond the archipelago. In Buzzard Bay I met Bill Kornblum, who was bringing his catboat *Victor* back to Greenport, New York, and decided to accompany him.

Now I was by myself again, on course to the most easterly island in New York State, approaching it from Newport, Rhode Island, with a strong southwest wind in a choppy sea. It was a cloudy July day, the gusty breeze changing directions at times while the boat cut through the waves like a threshing machine. Sailing south by southwest, I had to keep the boat close on the wind, and *Sojourn* was leaning hard, straining my arms as I attempted to hold the rudder steady. Sailing close-hauled isn't the fastest way, but it was either that or fall off course and tack back to Point Judith, about twelve miles west of Newport. After finally spotting the lighthouse on the tip of Narragansett, I was relieved to change to a more westerly course, sailing half-wind, faster and calmer. From here to the entrance of the Fisher Island Sound it was still another twenty nautical miles, which I calculated would take me another four-and-a-half hours if the wind remained steady.

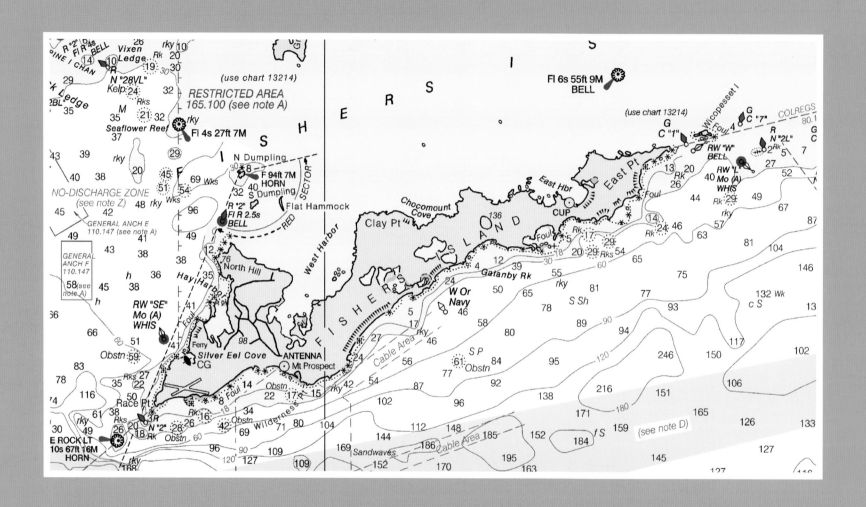

Although these waters don't technically belong to the archipelago of New York, in a larger geographical sense they are an essential part of the region. The most easterly islands—Fishers, Gull, Little Gull, and even Block Island—are part of the end moraine that shaped the New York Harbor and Long Island Sound. Adriaen Block, who explored, mapped, and named most of these islands was the first to describe them as a single archipelago. Fishers (Vishers) Island was named after one of Adriaen Block's crew members in 1614. With the borders between states ill-defined, the right to the island remained the cause for many battles between the states of Connecticut and New York. In 1640, the provision that Connecticut remain Fishers Island's rightful owner was crucial to the island's lease being given to the son of the governor of the Massachusetts Bay Colony and founder of the city of Boston, John Winthrop. But the border dispute lasted until 1879, when a joint commission with representatives from both states declared that it belonged to Southold, Long Island.

The entrance to Fishers Island Sound is a narrow channel through reefs and rocks marked by buoys with funny names like Sugar and Lord's Passage. I was heading toward the third, the Watch Hill entrance, where a gong and a bell would help navigate even in the worst weather. Still more than an hour away from the island, the sky was clear and the forecast was good. But as I approached the southwestern point of Rhode Island, where the strait into Fishers Island begins, the clouds grew darker. Within a few minutes, the buoys at the horizon already in sight, I was in the middle of a torrential rain storm, drenched to the bone, and heavy gusts of wind were pushing me toward the rough waters of the Watch Hill passage.

I found myself in a dense fog. I could not see farther than a hundred feet, so I turned the boat into the wind, switched on the engine, pulled down the sheets, and went in narrow circles, waiting. It is amazing how fast the weather can change on the water. Sometimes unannounced, out of nowhere, dark clouds appear, the wind changes, and before you know it, you're in the midst of a heavy thunderstorm. Sailing the archipelago of New York, experience has taught me that the whole thing often only lasts for half an hour, with the sun breaking through the clouds as if nothing had happened.

Being alone on a small boat in bad weather puts things into perspective for me. It forces a realistic evaluation of the situation and my own capability. There is no one to blame if I make a mistake, and so I have learned to question myself constantly before I act. Do I really know the right thing to do? This turns out to be one of the best things I have learned on the water: not knowing. Realizing my weaknesses made me stronger.

With that in mind I kept circling, studying the charts on my iPad in its waterproof case as best I could in this weather. It was only six p.m., and there were still a few hours of daylight left to get to Fishers Island once this rain storm was over. Sure enough, within twenty minutes the rain stopped, the sky cleared, and I passed safely into Fishers Island Sound. Soon I was approaching the island's small West Harbor. Looking back, the dark clouds still hung dramatically over the water, but in front of me the sun had started to set. I don't imagine that the approach to the island has changed much since 1729, when a young boy named Broteer from Dukandarra, Guinea, ended his odyssey from Africa on Fishers Island. The oldest son of a prince, he and his family were taken prisoner after his father was murdered by an invading army and sold to slave traders who put the little boy on a ship to Rhode Island. Rechristened "Venture," the boy was sold to George Mumford, who had rented Fishers Island from the Winthrop family and ran a commercial farm on the property. Venture spent more than thirteen years with the Mumford family, serving George and his son.

By the outbreak of the Revolutionary War, more than 20,000 slaves served white farmers and rich families in New York, more than half of them on Long Island, making one of five people on the East End of African descent.

Of the twelve million African captives enslaved in America, only a dozen kept a personal journal. Venture, who grew up on Fishers Island, was one of them. In his memoir, entitled *A Narrative of the Life and Adventures of Venture, A Native of Africa, But Resident above Sixty Years in the United States of America, Related by Himself*, he wrote about his time on Fishers Island:

"One day in particular, the authority which my master's son had set up, had like to have produce melancholy effects. For my master having set me off my business to perform that day and then left me to perform it, his son came up to me in the course of the day, big with authority, and commanded me very arrogantly to quit my present business and go directly about what he should order me. I replied to him that my master had given me so much to perform that day, and that I must therefore faithfully complete it in that time. He then broke out in a great rage, snatched a pitchfork and went to lay me over the head therewith; but I as soon got another and defended myself with it, or otherwise he might have murdered me in his outrage."

After the brutal violence Venture endured, he decided to escape, and with another man stole his master's boat and sailed to Montauk Point, only to be captured and resold to Stanton Thomas of Stonington, Connecticut. Here he once more was exposed to severe violence, but Venture never succumbed to the brutal force of his oppressors; instead he complained to the justice of peace. Again Venture was sold, this time to a small businessowner, Oliver Smith of Stonington, but Venture's wife and daughter remained with Stanton Thomas. Smith allowed him to earn money on his own to eventually pay for his freedom.

"I hired myself out at Fishers Island, and earned twenty pounds; thirteen pounds six shillings of which my master drew for the privilege, and the remainder I paid him for my freedom. This made fifty-one pounds two shillings which I paid him."

Freed at last, Venture adopted the last name of the master that let him go and went on to become a successful businessman, eventually paying for the freedom of his wife and children as well. They lived and died in Connecticut; Venture never visited Fishers Island again.

FROM HEART TO HART

At first I wasn't sure if the shapes that appeared on the horizon line were the first hint of the Manhattan skyline or merely a *fata morgana*, an optical illusion that sometimes occurs due to atmospheric conditions.

Fata Morgana is the Italian name of Morgan le Fay, the sorceress in the King Arthur saga, who sailors believed was responsible for the images of castles appearing in the air above the strait of Messina between Sicily and Italy that disoriented them and often lured them to their death.

Taking a closer look from the cockpit over the bow of the boat, I reassured myself that I was indeed looking at the tips of the Manhattan skyscrapers, although from so far away they looked more like the outline of a giant imaginary castle that could make a sailor's tale.

Behind me, the sun was rising. I had just past Matinecock Point about two miles from Glen Grove at nine a.m., running west. Due to the current, *Sojourn* was cutting smoothly through the calm water at six knots with the motor only at half throttle.

The coastline, with its soft hills and sandy beaches nestled around small bays overlooked by grand houses, could easily make me forget that I was approaching a metropolis of eight million people. At the same time, sighting the first sliver of the city excited me, filling me with a feeling of homecoming after I had spent the last couple of weeks sailing along the Sound.

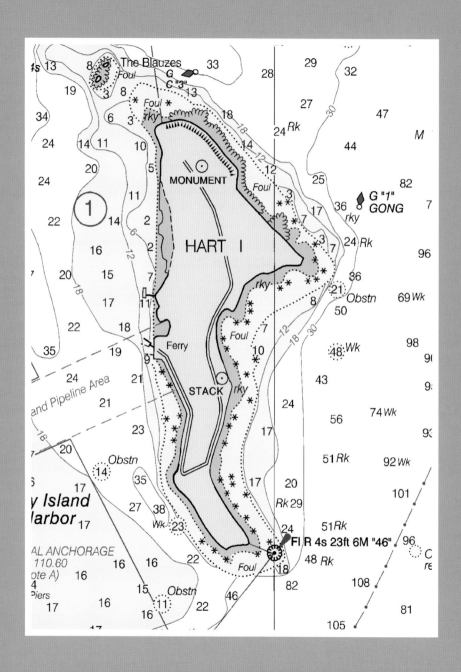

But the peaceful landscape around me was deceptive. I had to remind myself that the Execution Rocks Light was there for a reason, guiding ships through reefs and rocks that had been a dagger of death for umpteen ships over the centuries. They were smashed to pieces and sank in this area; countless people desperately tried to reach the safety of the shore, but drowned and sank to the bottom of the sea. Despite the picture-postcard bay, this really was a dark place. Even today, record audiences tune in to stories on cable TV about ghosts haunting the decommissioned lighthouse that serves as the only waterside bed and breakfast in the New York area. Nobody knows if the stories that gave this lighthouse its name are true, but it's said that during the Revolutionary War the British chained prisoners to the nearby rocks at low tide to await the cruel death that came with the rising water.

Passing the lighthouse uneventfully, I tacked toward Hart Island at the entranceway of New York City. From far off, I could already see the words: "PRISON - KEEP OFF!" written on a building on the west side of the island in large white letters.

On old British charts, this island was named for its shape: Heart Island. A name too nice for what has always been a place of sorrow, soon the letter e vanished like some of the unfortunates who awaited their fate on this windswept island. Now called Hart Island, it served as a prison during the Civil War for nearly 3,500 captured Confederate soldiers, and in 1868, New York City purchased the site for its "potter's field," where the bodies of the unknown are buried to this day. Since 1895, the island has been under the jurisdiction of the New York Department of Corrections, so often it fell to prisoners from nearby Rikers Island to serve as undertakers for the stream of unclaimed bodies from the city morgue, filling the vast cemetery with more than a million souls.

Heart Island. A name too nice for what has always been a place of sorrow, soon the letter e vanished like some of the unfortunates who awaited their fate on this windswept island.

Hardly any New Yorkers knew about this until the artist Melinda Hunt visited the island in 1996. She photographed how inmates from Rikers sank simple pine coffins into trenches. Some of these coffins were only the size of a shoebox; the prisoners were laying stillborn babies to rest. Since they have no birth certificates, these bodies have no death certificates, either, and so they can't be buried in any cemetery except Hart Island.

When Hunt first visited Hart Island, she discovered files stored in rusty cabinets housed under leaky roofs, although countless records were already destroyed by fire or mold. She initiated an inquiry through the Freedom of Information Act, receiving data about the bodies in the Hart Island trenches and making the information public via an online database. Through this work, some of the anonymous bodies now have names, and some of their loved ones finally know what happened to those who disappeared. One more result of Hunt's painstaking work: relatives can now visit a non-denominational chapel on the island.

Having passed City Island, I turned under the Throgs Neck Bridge into the East River. Airplanes approaching LaGuardia Airport on the port side flew low, their noise disrupting the tranquility that had reigned over my last few hours on Long Island Sound. The smell of kerosene mixed into other indefinable city odors when I passed the prison barge, tied up opposite Rikers Island with 800 inmates aboard. One of the largest prison complexes in the world, Rikers houses 10,000 inmates on any given day. I watched a few of them jogging in the caged outdoor space on top of the barge in the early morning sun, glancing through the fence down at my lonely sailboat as it passed by.

40°47.98'N - 073°53.31'W

DANTE'S INFERNO ON THE EAST RIVER

The East River current pulling me toward the Battery was still weak. So instead of using the channel between North and South Brother Islands, I passed North Brother on its west side, allowing me to take a good look at the old Ferry Terminal and the dilapidated hospital buildings that now serve as nesting grounds for barn swallows, great egrets, or American oystercatchers. Huge oil tanks connected to above-ground pipelines, truck-loading stations, and gray concrete warehouses on the Bronx shoreline contrast starkly with the lush green trees of the island, a nature at odds with the man-made stretch of industrial structures, a web of utility lines and sewer pipes that made it look like the service backyard for Manhattan. A strong smell from the Ward Island Waste-water Plant wafted from the southwest, and I wondered what this part of the city had looked like more than a hundred years ago when the owner of the Yankees, Jacob Ruppert, had his vacation house on South Brother, just a few hundred feet east from where I was right now.

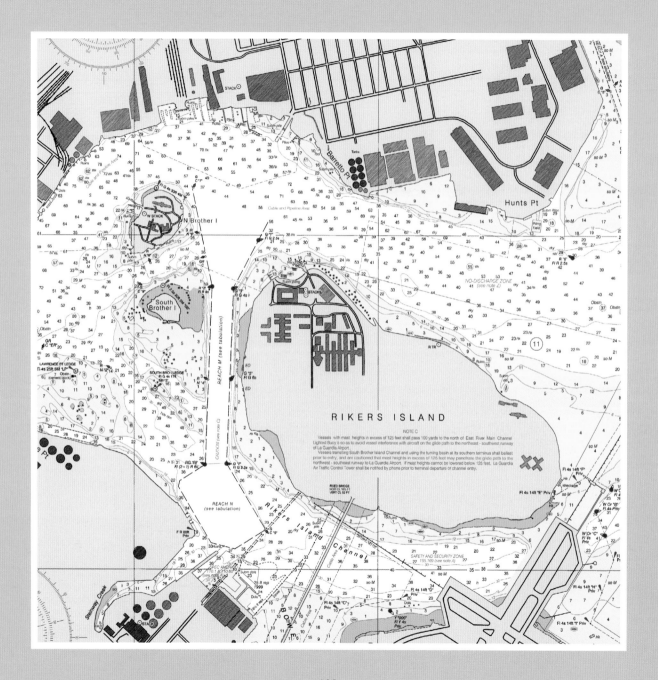

When that house burned down in 1909, it signified the end of all attempts to make these islands places to relax and enjoy nature. After Ruppert left, the islands that the Dutch called *De Gesellen*, from which the English translation "brother" derives, assumed a bleak history, just like many others of the archipelago. At the time, North Brother was already home to the Riverside Hospital, specializing in the treatment of smallpox and other highly contagious diseases that required patients to be quarantined. Mary Mallon, better known as Typhoid Mary, the first person in the US to suffer from typhoid fever without showing any symptoms, was hospitalized there and spent more than twenty years on North Brother Island before she died in 1938.

Since it was slack tide at Hell Gate, and I had plenty of time before the current turned against me, I decided to circle the islands' six acres. Ever since I learned about their existence in the East River, they have fascinated me. The idea that a sizable piece of habitable land remained unexploited in a city where space is the most valuable commodity is incredible. Its historic buildings are preserved, too.

An even more important reason for my interest, though, was perhaps my German heritage, because on a warm June day in 1904, a large part of what was called *Kleindeutschland* (little Germany) perished right there on the shore of this small island, after more than 1,400 members of the St. Mark's Church parish in the East Village boarded the steamboat *General Slocum* at nine a.m., mostly women and children excited

about the annual Sunday school picnic outing at Locust Grove on Long Island Sound. A couple of hours later, more than 1,000 of them were dead, either drowned in the river or burned to death in an uncontrollable fire that broke out in the lamp room of the thirteen-year-old steamboat. Before 9/11, this was the city's deadliest disaster. Worse yet, it could have been prevented.

The *General Slocum* fire was detected early on by a twelve-year-old boy. He alerted one of the ship's mates who, assuming the kid had just confused smoke and steam, dismissed the youngster's claim. When the deckhand finally realized that what was pushing out under the lamp room's door was indeed smoke, he had no idea what to do, because the crew hadn't had a fire drill in years. So, without much thought, he pushed open the door, feeding oxygen to the smoldering hay in which glasses were stored. Realizing his mistake, the mate panicked and wasted time looking for an officer for help. Captain Van Schaick had not been informed about the fire, as he was preparing *Slocum*'s dangerous passage through Hell Gate with his two pilots, maneuvering the ship through the heavy boat traffic on this summer Sunday.

When the deckhand finally returned to the lamp room, a reluctant officer in tow, the fire was a full-blown inferno, exploding from the stairway as from an open door of a furnace. The officer sent word to the bridge, but the captain, busy steering the ship through the rocks of Hell Gate, responded that he would come down as soon as possible. In the meantime, the two untrained crew rolled out the nearby fire hoses and prayed the pumps would work; in thirteen years they had never been serviced.

The two men were relieved when water from the emergency pumps brought the old hoses to life. But their relief was short-lived. The water pressure soon burst the old fabric hoses, and water rushed everywhere except through the nozzles of the fire extinguishers. Captain van Schaik, finally taking a look, realized in a split-second that his boat was lost. He rushed back to the bridge and directed the *Slocum* at full throttle aground on North Brothers Island. Another unfortunate mistake, and one that would bring the captain ten years in prison in the aftermath of the catastrophe, because he had decided to complete the carefully plotted passage through Hell Gate instead of steering to the nearest shore.

Below deck, the fire incinerated trapped men, women, and children. Others desperately grabbed life preservers, but these were of no help. Deliberately mal-produced, made from cork shavings rather than solid cork board, with the weight difference made up with metal, the vests weren't just useless, but once in the water turned into anchors that pulled the helpless victims down into the abyss of Hell Gate. By the time the *General Slocum* finally ran aground on the shore I was now looking at, most of the victims of this biggest maritime catastrophe, other than the sinking of the *Titanic*, had already died.

In the aftermath of the tragedy, the German community on the Lower East Side and the East Village fell apart, with some Germans moving to the Upper East Side and others leaving the city for good, and the former *Kleindeutschland* vanished. Much later, it was to become famous for the hippies and punks who have populated St. Mark's Place since the 1960s. The building's facade at 12 St. Marks still displays *Deutsch Amerikanische Schützengesellschaft* (German American Shooting Society). After the accident, 300 survivors came there to demand punishment for the federal inspectors who had failed to ensure the ship's safety equipment. Captain van Schaik alone was convicted, spending the next ten years in Sing Sing before being pardoned by President Taft on Christmas Day, 1912. Today, the building is home to a yoga school.

I turned into the narrow channel between the North and South Brother Islands and took in the city skyline, framed under the arch of the Hell Gate Bridge. By now the current had picked up, steadily pushing south, and soon I was sailing at more than ten knots into the Battery of Lower Manhattan.

40°42.12'N - 074°01.00'W
CITY OF THE MANHATTOES

Sailing into New York Harbor, the first thing I noticed was that the water color was changing. The closer I got to the Battery, the darker the gray-green shade—murky and mysterious. Throughout my journey around the New York archipelago, the water had taken on different personalities. At times it was gentle, friendly, and calm, and other times angry, rebelling, and violent, but no matter which of those conditions prevailed, they all had one thing in common: an unfailing memory. These waters record everything that had ever happened to them.

Entering the Battery was like looking into a wise old man's face, where each line in the leathery skin tells a life story. Scars speaking of injuries and pain, wrinkles sculpted by sorrow and grief morphing into traces of laughter and joy, clear and open eyes revealing sagacity, knowledge, and awareness.

Entering the Battery was like looking into a wise old man's face, where each line in the leathery skin tells a life story.

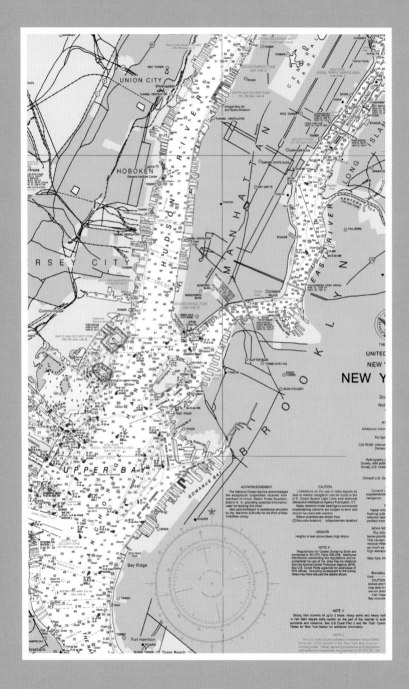

The water was speaking to me, and for the first time I started to understand what it had to say. Gliding along the Battery under full sail, I saw what Herman Melville had described in the opening chapter of *Moby Dick* more than 170 years ago:

"There now is your insular city of the Manhattoes, belted round by wharves as Indian isles by coral reefs—commerce surrounds it with her surf. Right and left, the streets take you waterward. Its extreme downtown is the battery, where that noble mole is washed by waves, and cooled by breezes, which a few hours previous were out of sight of land. Look at the crowds of water-gazers there."

Suddenly I understood why, throughout time, people have gazed at the water in awe. Not only does it symbolize the unknown or promise adventure, but in some way water holds the answers to life itself.

New York is as unthinkable without the sea as life would be without water, and if it wasn't for the protected natural New York Harbor, America would not be the country it is today.

The water between the Battery and Governors Island whispered to me that it had been there 18,000 years ago, when melting glaciers pushed the land into the sea and formed the North River delta. As I sailed closer to the city, the soundtrack changed: a cacophony of car engines, ambulance sirens, and music bleeding into the steady hum of the wind in the sails.

Sojourn was heeling heavily in the morning breeze with the sun still rising in the east, lighting Manhattan's skyline and putting a spotlight on the face of Lady Liberty, which the French have given not only to New York, but to America. The Statue of Liberty has greeted millions of immigrants who left everything behind and became the bedrock of the country they now call home. Listening to the water that splashes on the shore of Liberty's very own island, it dawned on me, an immigrant myself, that my journey into the New York archipelago was simply an attempt to map the territory; understanding the geography of the place where I live is essential for feeling who I am.

I had to pay attention to the ferries and barges that even at this early hour busily crisscrossed the shores of New Jersey, Liberty and Ellis Islands, and the Battery. New York is still a working harbor, even though the commercial docks on Manhattan's East and West sides are mostly gone. Still, container ships bring goods from all around the world to the Port of New York and New Jersey Container Terminal, now tucked away in the Newark Bay, reachable only through the Kill van Kull, a small strait between Staten Island and Bayonne.

The Statue of Liberty has greeted millions of immigrants who left everything behind and became the bedrock of the country they now call home.

Tacking back and forth between Manhattan, Long Island (with its New York city boroughs of Queens and Brooklyn), and Governors, Liberty, Ellis and Staten Islands, I realized that living on islands shapes people in a special way. Islanders have a unique personality determined by their limited living space and their separation from other islands or the mainland, resulting in a certain self-centeredness that clearly characterizes Manhattanites. With Brooklyn today inhabited by young professionals, it is hard to imagine that little more than twenty years ago, moving across the river was like leaving for a remote town in the Midwest; that was a typical islander attitude, with territory and identity strongly connected and often neglecting the disconnected land, no matter how far or near it may be. This explains why only a small group of urban historians and sailors, who are often foreigners like me, look at the city differently than the natives do, and recognize the island world that envelopes Manhattan.

September 11, 2001, would change that within a few hours. When the attacks that brought down the towers and killed 2,977 people resulted in the closure of all bridges, tunnels, and subway lines, millions of people realized in an instant that they were trapped on an island. Many desperately sought a means of escape. Most left Manhattan by foot, but as many as 500,000 were taken by boat to New Jersey or Brooklyn — a painful way to discover Manhattan's place in the vast archipelago.

Newly created public spaces, like the Hudson River Park in Manhattan and the Brooklyn Bridge Park on the western tip of Long Island, are evidence of a newly formed relationship with the water after 9/11.

Sailing along the renovated docks on the west side, taking a closer look, I could still detect the remains of the old working waterfront that for centuries defined the island's outer skin. Ruled by the hard work of longshoremen loading and unloading the vessels tied to terminals and brutally reigned by a lowlife mob, New Yorkers had turned their back on the dark and dirty waterfront with its shady bars, flophouses, and brothels.

The magnificent mansions around Central Park are a testament to this day that the wealthy New Yorkers all but forgot that Manhattan was an island surrounded by water. Whoever could afford it acquired a view focused on the middle of the island. The water was left to be exploited, with every pollutant thinkable washed into the island's veins by growing industry on the city's shores, killing almost everything that lived in the dark abyss of the underwater valleys.

Oysters, once abundant in New York and the poor man's food in the Big Apple for decades, almost completely disappeared. Joseph Mitchell's masterpiece, *The Bottom of the Harbor,* published in 1951 and lying next to my berth in *Sojourn*'s underbelly, tells the story. By mid-century, the New York waters were so poisoned that whatever lived in them was no longer safe for consumption. Bay men, clam diggers, and fishermen desperately clung to their professional lives while the water around New York was all but dead.

Those days of heavy pollution are long gone. The city has invested millions of dollars in new and modern sewage treatment plants that have all but stopped spilling waste into New York Harbor. Only on rare days of extended heavy rain, when the capacity of those plants is exceeded, does the sewer overflow system gush raw sewage into the bay, and that is washed out to sea by the tide.

However, decades of neglect and abuse have left the water extremely polluted. The 3.5-mile-long Newtown Creek that flows into the East River, and the Gowanus Canal north of the Brooklyn Marine Terminal, are so contaminated that they pose an imminent health risk to people, and the US Environmental Protection Agency deemed them Superfund sites, giving them the highest priority on the list of places to be cleaned up. The poison sits mostly in the sediment of the straits, and one of the biggest challenges that scientists face is the risk of releasing the pollutants into the water once the sediment containing it is disturbed.

Oysters are now helping to clean up the mess. Students at the New York Harbor School, a specialized maritime high school founded in Bushwick, Brooklyn, when it was still a working-class neighborhood, and now on Governor's Island, are the force behind the Billion Oyster Project. Each year these future marine biologists, oceanographers, and tugboat captains raise ten million oysters and plant them into the New York estuary. Each can purify approximately fifty gallons of water per day.

Through my journey around the archipelago of New York, I have learned to treasure the water. It is no longer just the element that carried my boat. Observing how different the water is at various places, and how it reacted to the environment it is part of, I started to fundamentally rethink my relationship with the aquatic world. Scientists in all disciplines have agreed that mankind's future hinges on the oceans, the single largest food source for a growing world population; and that environmental abuse is directly connected to climate change and the rising sea levels that threaten the very vista I am enjoying at this very moment.

New York shares its exposed position on the shore with many major cities of the world. Rising sea levels are a tangible threat to the New York Islands. Hurricane Sandy, in 2012, brought home in a painful way how a surge just a few feet above the regular tide can bring devastating destruction. An island surrounded by concrete bulkheads does not give the water any space to expand, and the inundation of city structures is the logical consequence. After Sandy, the city and the state of New York initiated a process to rethink how the metropolis can be better protected. Urban planners and architects have created a fascinating new city design with wetlands surrounding the island of Manhattan that would allow the water to be absorbed at high tides.

So far those plans have not been implemented, and the heavy harbor traffic created a slew of waves. *Sojourn* bobbed up and down, slamming its bow into the water even at low speed. Though under sail, I had to give way to every commercial vessel and was often forced to change course, slowing the boat down.

None of that really mattered, because approaching the city from the water in a small sailing vessel is a thrilling experience. Looking at the magnificent skyline with its high-rises that nineteenth-century sailors christened skyscrapers, I felt both part of this incredible urban energy and an outside observer. From this vista, Manhattan appeared to be built on a swimming platform, growing out of the water with just a thin gray line separating the water from the land. Like a materialized Fata Morgana, New York is difficult to grasp, with so many different people and their stories, viewpoints and ideas, dreams and tragedies all on one small island. Often contradicting each other, this orchestra of minds creates the symphony of a modern city for me. Drawn by a magnetic power, I slowly came closer and closer to shore and finally sailed into the mooring field at Pier 25, where *Grand Bank*, a 1942 schooner and floating restaurant berths during the summer months. Cutting gently through the calmer waters toward the dock, I climbed up to the bow with the boat hook in my hand, ready to grab the line, to tie up, and be home again.

Through my journey around the archipelago of New York, I have learned to treasure the water.

Thomas Halaczinsky is an award-winning New York documentary filmmaker, photographer, and writer who divides his time between Brooklyn and Greenport on Long Island's North Fork, where he keeps his thirty-foot sailboat *Sojourn*. His work focuses on the relationship between people and places. In documentary films such as *Coney Island: A Last Summer* (for German/French broadcaster ARTE in 2008) and *Don't Call It Heimweh*, the opening film of the 2005 Berlin Jewish Film Festival, he explored the importance of place for the identity of the protagonists. In 1996 he won an ACE award for his contribution to the EMMY-awarded film *Calling the Ghost*. In 2016 his photographic series "Archipelago New York," featured in this book, received an honorable mention at the Tokyo International Photo Award.